LLEWE

2 0

Witches'
Spell-A-Day
Almanac

Holidays & Lore
Spells, Rituals & Meditations

Copyright 2015 Llewellyn Worldwide Ltd.
Cover Design: Lisa Novak
Editing: Andrea Neff
Background photo: © PhotoDisc
Interior Art: © 2011, Steven McAfee
pp. 13, 33, 53, 73, 91, 109, 127, 147, 167, 185, 205, 225
Spell icons throughout: © 2011 Sherrie Thai

You can order Llewellyn books and annuals from *New Worlds*,
Llewellyn's catalog. To request a free copy of the catalog, call toll-free
1-877-NEW WRLD or visit our website at www.llewellyn.com.

ISBN: 978-0-7387-3399-9

Llewellyn is a registered trademark of Llewellyn Worldwide Ltd.
2143 Wooddale Drive
Woodbury, MN 55125

Printed in the United States of America

Contents

About the Authors

Peg Aloi is a media studies scholar, writer, singer, and professional gardener. She was the Media Coordinator for *The Witches' Voice* from 1997 through 2008. Her blog, *The Witching Hour* (www.patheos.com/blogs/themediawitches), focuses on Paganism and media. With her writing partner, Hannah Johnston, Peg co-organized two academic conferences at Harvard University on Paganism and the media. Their second book, *Carnivale and the American Grotesque: Critical Essays on the HBO Series*, has just been published by McFarland.

Blake Octavian Blair is an eclectic Pagan, ordained minister, shamanic practitioner, writer, Usui Reiki Master-Teacher, tarot reader, and musical artist. Blake blends various mystical traditions from both the East and West along with a reverence for the natural world into his own brand of modern Neo-Paganism and magick. Blake holds a degree in English and Religion from the University of Florida. He is an avid reader, crafter, and practicing vegetarian. Blake lives with his beloved husband, an aquarium full of fish, and an indoor jungle of houseplants. Visit him on the web at www.blakeoctavianblair.com or write him at blake@blakeoctavianblair.com.

Thuri Calafia is the author of *Dedicant: A Witch's Circle of Fire* and *Initiate: A Witch's Circle of Water*. She is an ordained minister, a Wiccan High Priestess, a teacher, and the creator of the Circles system and school. She is currently working on the third book in the Circles series, *Adept: A Witch's Circle of Earth*, and attends college full-time. She lives in the Pacific Northwest with her beloved Labrador, Miss Briana Fae.

Emily Carlin is an eclectic Witch, teacher, mediator, and attorney based in Seattle. She specializes in shadow magick and defensive magick. Emily teaches online at Shadowkrafting.com and at in-person events in the Puget Sound area. For more information, go to http://about.me/ecarlin.

Dallas Jennifer Cobb practices gratitude magic, giving thanks for her magical life, happy and healthy family, meaningful and flexible work, and joyous life. She believes the Goddess will provide time, energy, wisdom, and money to accomplish all her deepest desires. She lives in paradise, in a waterfront village in rural Ontario, and chants: "Thank you, thank you, thank you." Contact her at jennifer.cobb@live.com.

Kerri Connor is the High Priestess of the Gathering Grove. She has written several magic books, including *Spells for Tough Times*.

Raven Digitalis (Missoula, MT) is the author of *Shadow Magick Compendium*, *Planetary Spells & Rituals*, and *Goth Craft*, all published by Llewellyn. He is a Neopagan Priest and cofounder of an Eastern Hellenistic nonprofit community temple called Opus Aima Obscuræ (OAO). Also trained in Eastern philosophies and Georgian Witchcraft, Raven has been an earth-based practitioner since 1999, a Priest since 2003, a Freemason since 2012, and an empath all his life. He holds a degree in anthropology from the University of Montana and is also a professional Tarot reader, DJ, small-scale farmer, and animal rights advocate. Visit him at www.ravendigitalis.com, www.facebook.com/ravendigitalis, or www.facebook.com/ravendigitalisauthor.

Ellen Dugan is an award-winning author known as the "Garden Witch." A psychic-clairvoyant, she has been a practicing Witch for over twenty-seven years. She is a Master Gardener and teaches classes locally and online on Witchery, psychic development, and magick. She is the author of sixteen nonfiction books published by Llewellyn. *Legacy of Magick* is her first novel and was released in February 2015.

Michael Furie (Northern California), author of the books *Spellcasting for Beginners* and *Supermarket Magic*, has been a practicing Witch for over nineteen years. An American Witch, he practices in the Irish tradition and is a priest of the Cailleach. He has also written articles about magic and spirituality for online Pagan websites such as www.witchvox.com. Michael enjoys cooking, reading, studying herbalism, magic, Irish lore, and growing herbs. You can find him online at www.michaelfurie.com.

James Kambos became interested in magic and spellwork by watching his Greek grandmother perform folk magic that she learned as a child in Greece. He is also an artist and lives in Ohio.

Mickie Mueller is an award-winning and critically acclaimed artist of fantasy, fairy, and myth. She is an ordained Pagan minister and has studied Natural Magic, Fairy Magic, and Celtic tradition. She is also a Reiki Master/Teacher in the Usui Shiki Ryoho tradition. She enjoys creating magical art full of fairies, goddesses, and beings of folklore. She works primarily in a mix of colored pencil and watercolor infused with magical herbs corresponding to her subject matter. Mickie is the illustrator of *The Well Worn Path* and *The Hidden Path* decks, the writer/illustrator of *Voice of the Trees: A Celtic Divination Oracle*, and the illustrator of the

Mystical Cats Tarot. Mickie is a regular article contributor to several of the Llewellyn annuals. Visit her online at www.mickiemuellerart.com.

Charlynn Walls holds a BA in anthropology, with an emphasis in archaeology. She is an active member of her local community. She is now co-hosting a monthly discussion group in the Saint Louis area with Ellen Dugan. Charlynn teaches by presenting at various local festivals on a variety of topics. She continues to pursue her writing through articles for *Witches & Pagans* magazine, several of the Llewellyn annuals, and her blog, *Sage Offerings*, at www.sageofferings.net.

Tess Whitehurst is a feng shui consultant, intuitive counselor, and award-winning author. Her books include *Magical Housekeeping, The Good Energy Book, Magical Fashionista, The Art of Bliss,* and *The Magic of Flowers.* Learn about her work and sign up for her free monthly newsletter at www.tesswhitehurst.com.

Charlie Rainbow Wolf is happiest when she's creating something, especially if it can be made from items that others have cast aside. She is passionate about writing and is deeply intrigued by astrology, tarot, runes, and other divination oracles. Knitting and pottery are her favorite hobbies, although she happily confesses that she's easily distracted by all the wonderful things that life has to offer. Charlie is an advocate of organic gardening and cooking, and lives in the Midwest with her husband and her special needs Great Danes. Visit her at www.charlierainbow.com.

Natalie Zaman is a regular contributor to various Llewellyn annuals. She is the co-author of the Graven Images Oracle deck (Galde Press) and writes the recurring feature "Wandering Witch" for *Witches & Pagans* magazine. Her work has also appeared in *FATE, Sage Woman,* and *newWitch* magazines. When she's not on the road, she's chasing free-range hens in her self-sufficient and Pagan-friendly back garden. Find Natalie online at http://nataliezaman.blogspot.com or at http://broomstix.blogspot.com, a collection of crafts, stories, ritual, and art she curates for Pagan families.

A Note on Magic and Spells

The spells in the *Witches' Spell-A-Day Almanac* evoke everyday magic designed to improve our lives and homes. You needn't be an expert on magic to follow these simple rites and spells; as you will see if you use these spells throughout the year, magic, once mastered, is easy to perform. The only advanced technique required of you is the art of visualization.

Visualization is an act of controlled imagination. If you can call up in your mind a picture of your best friend's face or a flag flapping in the breeze, you can visualize. In magic, visualizations are used to direct and control magical energies. Basically the spellcaster creates a visual image of the spell's desired goal, whether it be perfect health, a safe house, or a protected pet.

Visualization is the basis of all good spells, and as such it is a tool that should be properly used. Visualization must be real in the mind of the spellcaster so it allows him or her to raise, concentrate, and send forth energy to accomplish the spell.

Perhaps when visualizing you'll find that you're doing everything right, but you don't feel anything. This is common, for we haven't been trained to acknowledge—let alone utilize—our magical abilities. Keep practicing, however, for your spells can "take" even if you're not the most experienced natural magician.

You will notice also that many spells in this collection have a somewhat "light" tone. They are seemingly fun and frivolous, filled with rhyme and colloquial speech. This is not to diminish the seriousness of the purpose, but rather to create a relaxed atmosphere for the practitioner. Lightness of spirit helps focus energy; rhyme and common language help the spellcaster remember the words and train the mind where it is needed. The intent of this magic is indeed very serious at times, and magic is never to be trifled with.

Even when your spells are effective, magic won't usually sparkle before your very eyes. The test of magic's success is time, not immediate eye-popping results. But you can feel magic's energy for yourself by rubbing your palms together briskly for ten seconds, then holding them a few inches apart. Sense the energy passing through them, the warm tingle in your palms. This is the power raised and used in magic. It comes from within and is perfectly natural.

Among the features of the *Witches' Spell-A-Day Almanac* are an easy-to-use "book of days" format; new spells specifically tailored for each day of the year (and its particular magical, astrological, and historical energies); and additional tips and lore for various days throughout the year—including color correspondences based on planetary influences, obscure and forgotten holidays and festivals, and an incense of the day to help you waft magical energies from the ether into your space. Moon signs, phases, and voids are also included to help you find the perfect time for your rituals and spells.

Enjoy your days, and have a magical year!

Spell–A–Day Icons

 New Moon

 Meditation, Divination

 Full Moon

 Money, Prosperity

 Abundance

 Protection

 Altar

 Relationship

 Balance

 Success

 Clearing, Cleaning

 Travel, Communication

 Garden

 Air Element

 Grab Bag

 Earth Element

 Health, Healing

 Fire Element

 Home

 Spirit Element

 Heart, Love

 Water Element

Spells at a Glance by Date and Category*

	Health	Protection	Success	Heart, Love	Clearing, Cleaning	Home	Meditation, Divination
Jan.	10, 30	5, 27, 29	1, 3, 8	22	4, 15, 19, 25, 31	18	21
Feb.		1, 11, 16, 17	7	14, 20	3, 4, 6		27
March		3, 7, 30	4, 15	18	2, 6, 14, 27		20, 31
April	10, 21, 27	20, 23, 28	12	19	25, 29	14, 15	
May			16, 17, 27	2, 8, 26	29		4
June	5, 14, 15	6, 18	21, 27	1, 3, 12, 17	29		
July	23	9, 12, 18			1, 3, 13, 27	30	7, 10, 16, 29
Aug.	14		31		3	5, 18	8, 23, 25
Sept.	5	23, 29	8, 10, 13	4		14	
Oct.	16	25, 28	18	4, 7	5, 21	15	3, 6, 20, 23
Nov.	3, 7, 19	9, 18	17	25		22, 26	16, 24
Dec.	1, 5, 6	8, 9	18, 27		19, 24	15, 21, 30	12

*List is not comprehensive.

2016

Year of Spells

January

B efore Julius Caesar hired the astronomer Sosigenes of Alexandria in 46
BCE to reform the calendar, the year began with the spring equinox.
But the traditional calendar had gotten out of sync with the seasons. The
new Julian calendar remained in effect until it, too, fell out of sync and was
reformed in 1582 by Pope Gregory XIII. The Gregorian calendar is today's
common calendar, though some religions still use variations of the Julian
calendar.

January is named for Janus (Ianus), the two-faced Roman god of the
doorway, which is the transition point between the safe indoors and the
outside world, where anything might happen. Before Janus came to the city,
he was Dianus, an Italian oak god whose consort was the woodland goddess
Diana. The Romans weren't alone in believing that this opening needed
to be protected. The mezuzah, which holds verses from Deuteronomy,
is affixed to doors of Jewish houses. Medieval cathedrals feature elaborate
façades around their doorways, and nearly every Pagan is taught to cut a
"doorway" into the energy of the circle.

When we do January magic, let's focus on openings, closings, and
transitions. What are we closing? What are we opening?

Barbara Ardinger, PhD

January 1
Friday

3rd ♏

☽ v/c 12:33 am

☽ → ♎ 1:41 am

Color of the day: Rose
Incense of the day: Cypress

New Year's Day – Kwanzaa ends

Sacred Good Luck Meal

Many cultures have a special meal that is considered lucky to eat on January 1. Depending on where you live, that lucky dish might be black-eyed peas and collard greens, ham hocks and beans, fish, lentils, or spicy posole.

Whatever your favorite lucky dish, prepare it according to tradition and boost its good luck with this spell. As you cook it, add the ingredients with awareness that foods have magical powers and each herb and ingredient adds unique properties. Be sure to stir clockwise with the intention of building up good vibes, and trace magical symbols into the pot or bowl with your spoon. Before you serve your meal, bless it:

Lucky meal, lucky year,

Build up joy, releasing fear.

All who dine on this blessed food

Shall have good luck the whole year through!

Serve the meal with love to your family and friends, and start off the year with a great tradition!

Mickie Mueller

NOTES:

January 2
Saturday

3rd ♎

4th Quarter 12:30 am

☽ v/c 11:23 am

Color of the day: Blue

Incense of the day: Sandalwood

A Spell for Calm and Peace

Today is the feast day of Saint Seraphim, a Russian monk and mystic known for his gentleness. This spell in his honor will help you achieve calm and peace.

You'll need a rose-quartz crystal and a pink candle. Light the candle and place the crystal in front of it. Relax as you gaze at the candle. Visualize a pink light coming from the crystal; let it surround you. Repeat this quote from Saint Seraphim three times:

Acquire a peaceful spirit, and around you thousands will be saved.

Snuff out the candle and relax again. As you go through the day and face a difficult person or situation, "see" that pink light surrounding you and remember the quote. Maybe the person you're dealing with is having a bad day; put yourself in their position. Think of your spell and turn on the charm. You'll be able to face anything.

James Kambos

 January 3
Sunday

4th ♎

☽ → ♏ 2:36 pm

Color of the day: Amber

Incense of the day: Marigold

Steady Success Ritual

Tonight marks the peak of the Quadrantids meteor shower. (Times and visibility will vary depending on your area and other variables.) Bootes, the constellation where the Quadrantids originate, is aligned with hard work, discipline, and boundary-setting. Arcturus, its principal star, is associated with protection, power, and prosperity.

Anoint a dark blue candle with essential oil of vetiver. Outside under the stars (or inside if necessary), hold the candle in both hands and say:

Arcturus, I align with you. Riding your wave of light, I protect the wealth and blessings I already have, and draw even more abundance into my life experience. I fully commit to, and work steadily toward, my goals. With clarity, focus, and energy, I successfully manifest my heart's truest desires into form. Thank you.

Visualize the candle and your entire body and aura being filled with radiant starlight. Place the candle on your altar and light it.

Tess Whitehurst

January 4
Monday

4th ♏

Color of the day: White
Incense of the day: Lily

A Spell for Letting Go

Having trouble sticking to your New Year's resolutions already? Try this. You'll need a black pen, sheets of white paper, and some kind of a fire—a yellow candle will suffice. Write down what resolutions you made and what you feel is blocking you from achieving them. Don't be surprised if this turns into an epistle—that's a good thing! You're purging what is standing in your way. Once you've written it all out, carefully burn the paper in the fire, saying:

With the power of me, I set thee free.

See all your obstacles leaving and making way for your determination. If you use the candle to burn the paper, then take the ashes outside somewhere off your property and dispose of them there. When you are tempted to break your vows, remember that you've removed the temptation and you're strong enough to stick to your word.

Charlie Rainbow Wolf

 ## January 5
Tuesday

4th ♏
☽ v/c 12:47 pm

Color of the day: Scarlet
Incense of the day: Geranium

Mars Charm Bag

Tuesday carries the energetic currents of its planetary ruler, Mars, and thus is also related to the god of war. If you notice some warlike currents floating among those you encounter today, you can protect yourself by making a protection charm bag.

Simply gather a small pouch, bag, or square of fabric, plus a small polished protective gemstone, such as black tourmaline, and any three of the following Mars-associated herbs: pine needles, allspice, basil, cumin, or tobacco. Concentrate on your intent for protection as you add each ingredient to the bag or fabric. After all ingredients have been added, close up the bag or tie up the corners of the fabric. Hold the bag and visualize a protective force field of energy being emitted from the bag. Chant three times:

Charm bag of Mars, protect me from warlike energy. Blessed be!

Carry the charm bag in a pocket or wear as a necklace.

Blake Octavian Blair

January 6
Wednesday

4th ♏

☽ → ♐ 1:56 am

Color of the day: Yellow
Incense of the day: Lilac

Persephone's Journey

The festival honoring Persephone was held on this day to recognize her descent into the Underworld, but also her eventual return. As night falls, set out your altar in honor of her. You might include whole pomegranates and seeds. The colors of the altar should be garnet and white. You should have two candles at the center, along with your favorite representation of the Death card from the tarot.

Sit in front of your altar and light one of the candles. The unlit candle represents the world that is dark and frozen as Persephone visits the Underworld. Now light the other candle. This represents Persephone's eventual return to the world and the impact her presence has on it. Sit quietly in contemplation of the Death card as a metamorphosis from what was to what will be.

Charlynn Walls

 ## January 7
Thursday

4th ♐

☽ v/c 9:44 pm

Color of the day: Purple
Incense of the day: Apricot

Spell to Rededicate Your Altar

First, make sure your altar is freshly cleaned and all your supplies are well organized. Ground and center and take your time to slowly cleanse your altar with sage, then purify it with saltwater. Say:

From this moment forward, my altar is dedicated to _____ (your personal matron goddesses and/or patron gods) and myself. I have meditated on my sacred purpose for myself and my altar, and now (as you waft incense smoke over the altar) I charge this altar to that purpose.

Dot your altar with anointing or spell-sealing oil, and say:

So mote it be.

Thuri Calafia

January 8
Friday

4th ♐

☽ → ♑ 10:07 am

Color of the day: Pink
Incense of the day: Rose

Fire Up for Success

You've been working on your New Year's resolutions for a week now. Is your enthusiasm starting to wane? Is it more difficult than you expected? Use this spell to fire up your attitude and help ensure success.

Write down any negative feelings you have about working on your resolutions. Is time a factor? Or willpower? What is holding you back from complete success?

Write down all of the obstacles. Light a green candle (green neutralizes difficult situations) and, using a fireproof container, burn the list with the candle. As you do so, say:

Take my negatives and burn them away.

Let them disappear and allow me to work toward my goals.

With positive thoughts and a positive mind,

I will reach my goals, I will attain my desires.

Fire me up for success.

So mote it be.

Kerri Connor

 # January 9
Saturday

4th ♑

New Moon 8:31 pm

Color of the day: Black
Incense of the day: Pine

Make Your Mark

Led Zeppelin's Jimmy Page (whose birthday is today!) is known for his occult interests as well as his guitar skills. "Zoso," his personal glyph, means "to invoke"— an essential element for new moon magic.

Create your own glyph by combining letters, numbers, symbols, and/or images that hold meaning for you. (For inspiration, look at the personal glyphs created by J.R.R. Tolkien and John Dee.) When you've perfected your design, draw the glyph on a clean piece of paper, visualizing yourself in the lines of each element as you work. Leave it outside or by a window to take in the energy of the new moon.

Keep your glyph active and alive: Trace it in the air with your finger or write it in your book of shadows to seal spells, and carve it into candles to infuse intentions with your spirit. Include it in any magical writing.

Natalie Zaman

January 10
Sunday

1st ♑

☽ v/c 12:39 pm

☽ → ♒ 3:23 pm

Color of the day: Orange
Incense of the day: Eucalyptus

Sweet Dreams

In the deep dark of winter, let us take time to engage the darkness and welcome our dreams—the magical language of the subconscious that speaks to us in sleep. Tonight, before bed, do a personal ritual to cultivate and stimulate your dreams. Plan a little feast of food and drink to sweeten the subconscious. Research shows that foods rich in vitamin B6 and tryptophan are linked with greater dream intensity and recall. Make a snack of chicken, turkey, or pumpkin seeds. Drink dairy, soy products, or chamomile tea. Savor your snack early in the evening, mindfully consuming and enjoying each sip and bite. Intone:

I sip to quench my eternal thirst,

I eat to feed my dreams,

I nurture divine possibility,

Knowing that what will be, will be.

Place paper and a pen next to your bed to write down the magical messages. Sweet dreams!

Dallas Jennifer Cobb

January 11
Monday

1st ♒

☽ v/c 8:09 pm

Color of the day: Ivory
Incense of the day: Clary sage

Using a Locket for Magic

Though I enjoy using charm bags, it's not always feasible or wise to carry bags of herbs, especially if you have to go anywhere with security; it'd be really awkward to explain a mojo bag to a guard at a government office, for example. A simple solution is to use a locket instead of a charm bag. Jewelry is usually much less conspicuous, and lockets have the advantage of being able to hold a photograph or other small item.

To use a locket magically, you can take a picture of something that is symbolic of your goal and place it in the locket. To charge it, hold the locket in both hands and say these or similar words:

Magical treasure, nexus point,

In you, through you, the force is drawn.

Talisman of power, I now anoint.

My goal is reached; it shall be done.

Repeat your specific goal three times.

Michael Furie

January 12
Tuesday

1st ♒

☽ → ♓ 6:53 pm

Color of the day: Red
Incense of the day: Bayberry

Creating a Wintertime Altar

For most of us who live in the Northern Hemisphere, the cold breath of winter surrounds us at this time of year. What better way to honor that energy than to create your own shrine of the season?

Christmas and the Yuletide have passed, but it's likely that some of your decorative seasonal supplies are still close at hand. To begin, cover a small table with a white cloth to represent snow, even if snow is not prevalent in your area (natural fabric is preferable). You may wish to construct the shrine outdoors—or even construct an altar from snow itself!

Dedicate the shrine to the Holly King, the aspect of the Neopagan God archetype made notable in the poetry of Robert Graves. Because the Holly King represents winter, decorate the shrine with snowmen, evergreen needles, images of snowflakes, candles, an effigy of Santa Claus (who is himself a Holly King), and anything that represents the season to you. Perform your magick and meditation at this special shrine until the spring equinox.

Raven Digitalis

 January 13
Wednesday

1st ♓

Color of the day: White
Incense of the day: Marjoram

Zephyr Communication Spell

Whenever it's especially important that someone understands what you have to say, you can call on zephyrs (the elementals of air) for aid. Recite the following incantation the morning before you speak:

> I call on the zephyrs of the air,
> come and heed my words.
>
> I must communicate with [person(s) you
> need clear communication with] today.
>
> [Person(s)] must hear my words
> and understand my intent.
>
> Help me to clear the air and
> be understood.
>
> Help me to listen and
> comprehend accurately.
>
> Help me to speak with eloquence
> and clarity.
>
> As I do will, so mote it be.

After you've spoken and received the zephyrs' aid, be sure to give them an offering in gratitude (they greatly enjoy incense). This will ensure their continuing goodwill.

Emily Carlin

January 14
Thursday

1st ♓

☽ v/c 11:31 am

☽ → ♈ 9:48 pm

Color of the day: Green
Incense of the day: Balsam

Simmering Pot of Prosperity

We all desire to keep the flow of prosperous energy moving in our lives. We also like to make our homes warm and inviting, both for ourselves and our guests. Using fragrant natural herbs and spices is an easy way to accomplish both goals at once!

Raid your kitchen spice rack or cabinet, and collect any three of the following: cinnamon, clove, nutmeg, allspice, and orange peel or zest. Add the three of your choosing (about one teaspoon of each) to a pot of water on your stove. Set the pot to simmer, uncovered, and recite the following:

Fragrant spice, bring all things nice.

Simmering, brewing, prosperity luring.

For the highest good! So mote it be!

Watch the pot to ensure safety. Replace the water when necessary, or remove the pot when desired and pour its contents onto the earth outside your home.

Blake Octavian Blair

January 15
Friday

1st ♈

Color of the day: Purple
Incense of the day: Mint

A Spell to Erase a Bad Memory

For this spell, you'll need a bathtub (a shower will also work), a rose quartz, some pink candles, and some nice body wash or shampoo (rose-scented is preferable, but any will work).

Light the candles and get into the water. Add the rose quartz—the water won't hurt it. Concentrate on what you want to forget, in all its painful glory. When the memory is fully fixated in your mind, pull the plug if you're in the bathtub or turn off the water if you're in the shower. Wait until the water has drained. Feel the weight of your thoughts draining away with the water as it leaves you, taking this bad memory with it. When you feel lighter, and the water is gone, pinch out the candles. If you find yourself starting to remember, just remind yourself that you've washed it out of your memory, and turn your thoughts elsewhere.

Charlie Rainbow Wolf

January 16

Saturday

1st ♈

☽ v/c 6:26 pm

2nd Quarter 6:26 pm

Color of the day: Brown

Incense of the day: Sage

Midwinter Spell for Focus

To take advantage of the quiet, dormant energy of winter, we need to tap into our inner depths and possibly kindle some heat and light there. For those who live in dark or cold climates in winter, depression and restlessness can set in. Maybe you're already exercising and getting outside to combat these effects, but a spell can help generate some focused energy.

Do this working at noon, when the sun is at its zenith. Even if it is not sunny out, look upward in the sky and try to sense the sun's position directly overhead. Close your eyes and imagine the heat and light of the sun on your face. Let that warmth and power flow over your face and down your body. Visualize yourself outdoors in summer doing the same thing and feeling the sun's intensity. Wrap your arms around yourself to "hold in" the sun's energy, and draw upon this when you feel the gloominess of winter setting in.

Peg Aloi

January 17

Sunday

2nd ♈

☽ → ♉ 12:48 am

Color of the day: Gold

Incense of the day: Hyacinth

Snow Queen Charm for Transformation

Wow, it's cold outside! Now is the perfect time to work some snow and ice magick. This spell calls on some of the classic winter goddesses who are associated with snow and ice. These three deities are rather fierce and fabulous ladies, so invoke their powers carefully, and remember that they bring transformation quickly and with no sympathy.

Bundle up and go outside. Stand in the elements and feel their force, then repeat this charm three times:

> *Known by many names, to the Snow Queen I hail,*
>
> *Berchta, Holda, Skadi, behind their snowy veil.*
>
> *May healthy transformation now swirl all around me,*
>
> *By winter's snow and ice, as I will, so mote it be!*

Ellen Dugan

January 18
Monday

2nd ♉

Color of the day: Silver
Incense of the day: Hyssop

Birthday of Martin Luther King Jr. (observed)

Kitchen Blessing

The hearth is the heart of the home, and throughout winter, it is a central place of comfort, nurturance, and gathering. Today, bless your hearth—bless your kitchen. Gather sage, matches, and a small sweet treat. In a fireproof container, light the sage, creating smoke. Gently fan it throughout your kitchen. As you smudge, say:

Smoke, gather, and purify, cleaning this space.

Open the window or door. Lean out and let the smoke rise up to the sky:

Carry my blessings to the heavens.

Moving back indoors, smudge your stove, the heart of the kitchen:

Bless this kitchen and all who are nourished here.

Eat the sweet treat, extinguish the smudge pot, and intone:

May this hearth nourish us and feed our spirits. Indeed, life is sweet.

Dallas Jennifer Cobb

NOTES:

January 19

Tuesday

2nd ☿

☽ v/c 1:50 am

☽ → ♊ 4:13 am

Color of the day: White
Incense of the day: Ylang-ylang

Break the Ice Spell

To cleanse your space or to break a habit, try this spell. You'll need a piece of paper, a blue ink pen, and a one-quart freezer bag. Begin by writing your problem or habit on the paper. Then place the paper in the freezer bag and add enough water to cover the paper. Put the bag in the freezer.

After the water has frozen, lay the bag on the kitchen counter. Using a rolling pin or hammer, hit the bag to break up the ice. Imagine your problem breaking up as you break the ice. After you've broken the ice, let it melt in the bag. Once the ice is melted, pour out the water and paper onto the ground or a compost pile. Bury the paper if you wish and walk away. Your problem will begin to fade.

James Kambos

 January 20

Wednesday

2nd ♊

☉ → ♒ 10:27 am

Color of the day: Brown
Incense of the day: Honeysuckle

Blessing Jar

Count your blessings and they will come back a hundredfold! To remember the good things that happen every day (and ensure that they keep coming), write this incantation on an empty bottle or jar:

Love, luck, health,

Happiness and wealth.

This is the spell I spin.

Double, treble what lies within!

Keep a pen and small pieces of paper (little sticky notes in bright colors work really well) near the jar. Every day, write down at least one thing that makes you happy, even if it's small, and fold or roll it up before tucking it inside. Once the jar is full, take out all your blessings and reread them. I put mine in my journal, but you can offer them up to the universe in a fire of gratitude. Watch more blessings roll in, and begin the process again!

Natalie Zaman

January 21
Thursday

2nd ♊

☽ v/c 3:01 am

☽ → ♋ 8:28 am

Color of the day: White
Incense of the day: Carnation

The Road Thus Far

It is three weeks into the new year. Take a moment to meditate and review how this time of new beginnings is working out for you. Get into a comfortable position and place a dab of diluted frankincense oil on your third eye. Use deep, even breathing to enter into a meditative state. Focus on the last three weeks, and think about the following questions:

What has been going well for you? What areas of your life need more work? What do you find motivates you? What concerns do you have? Where do you see yourself six months from now? A year from now? Focus on achieving your goals (even if things haven't been going great). Acknowledge any setbacks or interruptions and then move on. Visualize your goals being achieved. How do you feel? How have you changed by achieving these goals? Be the changes. Focus only on the positive and see yourself as if all your goals have already been accomplished.

Kerri Connor

 January 22
Friday

2nd ♋

Color of the day: Coral
Incense of the day: Yarrow

Drawing Love to You

We all want to be loved. If you are lacking a committed relationship, this spell just may draw the right type of person to you.

You will need a small bag or box. Create a list of specific qualities that you want to see in a potential partner. Keep the list concise. Next, pick an herb or a stone that corresponds to each quality you listed. As you add each item to the bag or box, say what it represents. After you have all of your items in the bag or box, place your list in with them and say:

Aphrodite, goddess of love, hear my plea. Bring to me my ideal partner. So mote it be.

Seal up the bag or box and place it beside your bed.

Charlynn Walls

January 23
Saturday

2nd ♋

☽ v/c 1:21 am

☽ → ♌ 2:21 pm

Full Moon 8:46 pm

Color of the day: Indigo
Incense of the day: Patchouli

Full Moon Spell for Health

After the holidays, when we tend to overindulge, we often strive to adopt a new health regimen. We can use the powerful energy that leads up to the full moon to begin new habits. Our physical vitality is very apparent at this time, and it is believed that our body's powers of absorption are at their strongest during the full moon.

On this day, eat lightly and only consume healthy, nourishing foods. When evening falls and the moon begins to rise, find a place where you can see the full moon in the sky (if it's cloudy, face the direction where the moon is rising). Picture the light of the moon glowing, and picture yourself glowing with health. Put some fresh fruit juice in a goblet, lift it to the moon, and drink it, saying:

I drink to my health and well-being.
I drink in the full moon's energy.
I allow this energy to strengthen my
resolve. I absorb health and vitality
from my food.

Do this spell as a reminder on each full moon to help you maintain healthy habits. Harness that potent full-moon energy to strengthen your resolve.

Peg Aloi

NOTES:

January 24

Sunday

3rd ♌

☽ v/c 9:51 pm

Color of the day: Yellow
Incense of the day: Heliotrope

Cutting Last Year's Ties

Spend some time in meditation prior to your spellwork, and decide which projects or relationships that you worked on last year must be let go of for your (or another's) greater good. Draw small pictures or symbols of those things you wish to leave behind on paper, or carve them into a small black candle. Tie a black string around your waist, and then tie strings: one end to the symbol you made, and the other end to the string around your waist, which symbolizes the bond and manifests the tie you'll be cutting in this rite. Take a moment to contemplate the energy you expended toward each goal or relationship, as well as what that energy pattern meant—or still means—to you. Acknowledge what it means to you to let that energy pattern go. When you find yourself becoming willing to truly let go, use a white-handled knife (or other appropriate tool) to cut each thread. Say:

I let you go in peace and love, and
I am grateful for what I learned.

Be blessed.

Thuri Calafia

January 25

Monday

3rd ♌

☽ → ♍ 10:46 pm

Color of the day: Gray
Incense of the day: Rosemary

Shake, Rattle, and Roll!

As we approach the end of January and the moon wanes, it seems like a great time to cast away any baneful energies that might be lingering from the previous year and the stress of the holiday season. Make some noise to drive out the baddies! Get a wooden spoon and bang on the bottom of a big pan, ring bells, shake a rattle, crank up some of your favorite music, and use sound to scare away any dark, musty vibes that are still lurking. Sound has a way of sending vibrations into every corner, nook, and cranny that smudging or asperging just can't reach. As you make your magical racket, do so with the intention that you're clearing out your house. Begin at one end of your home and work your way counterclockwise. Release and end by shooing any astral nasties right out the back door, shouting:

And stay out!

Mickie Mueller

January 26
Tuesday

3rd ♍

Color of the day: Black
Incense of the day: Cedar

Courageous Candle Spell

Tuesday is the day of the week associated with the planet Mars. Courage, bravery, and standing your ground are all themes to work on this day. Today is also a waning moon, a good time for removing obstacles.

Light a red votive candle and place it in a candle cup. Now focus on any obstacles in your path, and see them fading and becoming inconsequential. Then repeat this charm three times:

By the planet of Mars, I call for courage true.

Grant me valor and passion in all that I do.

As this red candle burns and melts away,

Obstacles to my success will now fade.

This spell candle will burn straight and true,

May I be blessed in all that I do.

Allow the candle to burn out in a safe place.

Ellen Dugan

January 27
Wednesday

3rd ♍

☽ v/c 7:11 pm

Color of the day: Topaz
Incense of the day: Lavender

Car Protection Cord

Lots of people have items hanging from the rearview mirror of their car: good-luck charms, religious medals, or just sentimental trinkets. We can use this practice to weave a subtle yet powerful bit of protection magic for our vehicle and ourselves.

To make this cord, you will need to charge a key or key-shaped charm by holding and visualizing it filled with protective white light, and have three lengths of black cord (about twelve inches each). Knot the cords at one end, and hold this knot between your teeth. Visualize your car and see it as having a clear but strong force field surrounding it. Transfer this picture into the cord as you braid the strands together. Tie seven more knots in the cord, about an inch and a half apart, to hold the power. Once you reach the end, add the key, tying one last knot to join both ends of the cord together. Hang on the rearview mirror.

Michael Furie

January 28
Thursday

3rd ♏

☽ → ♎ 9:59 am

Color of the day: Crimson
Incense of the day: Mulberry

Abundance Attitude Adjustment

To balance out and recalibrate your relationship with money, make four lists. First, list positive new habits you can adopt surrounding money, including every way to comfortably save money that you can think of: borrow books from the library, host clothing swaps, etc. Second, list things that you might responsibly spend money on that you have been neglecting, such as a new dish towel, car maintenance, or even something that seems like more of a luxury, such as bath salts or a color of lipstick that you like. Third, list your limiting beliefs about money, such as "rich people are unhappy" or "money is always a problem." Now make a fourth list by rewriting every limiting belief, transforming it into a positive one. Commit to making changes according to lists one, two, and four. Throw the third list onto a fire or burn it safely in a cauldron or pot.

Tess Whitehurst

January 29
Friday

3rd ♎

☽ v/c 8:34 pm

Color of the day: White
Incense of the day: Thyme

Mirror Protection Spell

Recite the following incantation to reflect negative energy back to the sender. This spell can be recited with eyes closed or in front of a black mirror.

*By the powers of the moon and sun,
I conjure.*

Let the power of the elements come to me.

Encircle me.

Unicorn of the north, come to me.

*I charge thee, lend me thy power
to ground.*

Griffin of the east, come to me.

*I charge thee, lend me thy power
of knowledge.*

Dragon of the south, come to me.

*I charge thee, lend me thy power
of protection.*

Serpent of the west, come to me.

*I charge thee, lend me thy power
of emotion.*

Thy powers encircle.

Thy powers wind, thrice round.

Let negative energy sent to me

Be sent back where it came times three.

Never let this charm reverse

Or upon me place a curse.

By nature's will and harm to none,

Let this, my charm, not be undone.

Emily Carlin

NOTES:

January 30
Saturday
3rd ♎︎

☽ → ♏︎ 10:50 pm

Color of the day: Gray
Incense of the day: Ivy

A Bedtime Spell for Renewal

It was Edgar Allan Poe who penned the words, "Sleep, those little slices of death…" It is interesting to think that a part of our consciousness dies (alongside many physical cells) during the process of sleep. For those of us who function with one foot in each world, as the witchy saying goes, it's of utmost importance to get proper and healthy sleep.

When you prepare for a night's sleep, see that a bowl of lavender sits next to you. Place a special amethyst stone in the center. Place another lavender/amethyst bowl in the westernmost quadrant of your room. Take three slow sniffs of the lavender next to you before setting the bowl down. Then lie down, cover up, close your eyes, and cross your arms across your chest (in the traditional Corpse Pose). Say aloud three times:

As I lay me down to rest, I ask for
renewal through the Gates of the West.

Visualize yourself surrounded in a lavender hue, and note how you feel when you awaken.

Raven Digitalis

January 31
Sunday
3rd ♏︎

4th Quarter 10:28 pm

Color of the day: Gold
Incense of the day: Almond

Soap, Opera, and a Shower

On this day in 1949, the first daytime-television soap opera was broadcast. The genre was so named because most of the programs' sponsors were soap companies and the shows' plots contained a level of melodrama often seen in traditional operas. The shows contained no traditional opera—and neither will this spell! However, taking a cue from the inspiration for the genre name, gather your favorite natural soap and head for the shower. Chant the following (or sing it operatically, if you'd prefer) while visualizing the soap energetically cleansing you of all detrimental energies:

Suds and lather, upon my body gather.

Energy of detriment and disarray,

May this soap wash away!

Swirling, whirling, down the drain,

You shall not cause any pain!

Blessed be—so mote it be!

Blake Octavian Blair

February

February is the second and shortest month of the year. Named after the Latin word *februum*, it means "purification." This corresponds with the purification ritual of Februa on the full moon, originally the 15th in the ancient Roman calendar. Do some late-winter or early-spring cleaning. Get the whole coven involved in cleaning the covenstead.

Foreign names reveal more. In Old English, February was called Solmonath, which means "mud month," or Kale-monath, which refers to cabbage. The Slovene name Svečan invokes Candlemas. The Finnish name Helmikuu means "month of the pearl," in which melting snow forms pearly drops of ice on the trees. In Polish this is Luty, the "month of ice," and in Czech it's Únor, when the river ice submerges. Native American names include Wolf Moon, Snow Moon, and Wind Moon.

This month is said to foreshadow the weather in the warm season. A wet February suggests a pleasant and fruitful summer. A dry, clear month hints at trouble to come. You can see echoes of this in Groundhog Day, where again foul weather predicts fair.

February honors Aradia, Brigid, and Juno Februa. It also features the Maiden Goddess and the consort God as Youth or Rogue.

Elizabeth Barrette

February 1
Monday

4th ♏

☽ v/c 7:35 pm

Color of the day: Lavender
Incense of the day: Narcissus

A Winter Protection Amulet

The days may be lengthening, but winter is still very much with us. This amulet will help protect you against the cold—from the elements or from cold-hearted people. You'll need a small square of red cotton fabric, some string to tie it shut, a pinch of salt, a pinch of sage, a pinch of juniper, and a pinch of garlic. Do this at the dark of the moon, if possible. Add the four ingredients to the center of the cloth, and tie it closed. As you do so, say these words:

Salt and juniper,

Garlic and sage,

Protect my journey

Against all rage.

Make one of these every year on February 1st to help protect your home. You can also place one in your vehicle for traveling in bad weather. An amulet carried in your purse or pocket works also to help you stay sure-footed, either physically or metaphorically.

Charlie Rainbow Wolf

February 2
Tuesday

4th ♏

☽ → ♐ 10:50 am

Color of the day: Gray
Incense of the day: Basil

Imbolc – Groundhog Day

Happy Imbolc!

We are at the halfway point between winter and spring. Today is the feast day of the goddess Brigid. Classic colors for this sabbat include white, purple, and gold. For this particular sabbat, I like to work with lots of candles. The most affordable way to do this is by working with tealights. The following spell calls on Brigid for illumination, creativity, and purpose.

Arrange as many tealight candles as possible in a safe, flat place. Be sure to keep them away from curious pets and small children! Light all of the candles, and as you do say, *Blessed be, Brigid*, or *Grant me creativity*, or *Grant me purpose.*

Once the candles are all lit and flickering, repeat this spell verse:

The great goddess Brigid was known by many names,

Breed, Brigit, and Bride—you are all one and the same.

On this Imbolc sabbat, I call you
by candlelight,

Bless me with creativity and purpose
this night.

By light and magick, this spell is spun,

For the good of all, with harm to none.

Allow the candles to burn out in a
safe place. Happy Imbolc!

Ellen Dugan

NOTES:

February 3
Wednesday

4th ♐

Color of the day: White
Incense of the day: Bay laurel

home Cleansing

Wednesday is a good day of the week for change, and what better time for a change, as we are starting a new year!

Take a little time today to change your environment. The winter months find us storing things that we really have no use for, so get rid of them. Make space for things that fulfill you. Once you get your physical space cleared, cleanse your home. Create a spray with a little sage and spearmint oil mixed with water. As you walk about your home spritzing the rooms, say:

I cleanse this home of the negative
so I can welcome change.

The sage will cleanse the space of any negativity, and the spearmint will help with prosperity and protection.

Charlynn Walls

February 4
Thursday

4th ♐

☽ v/c 5:04 am

☽ → ♑ 7:44 pm

Color of the day: Turquoise
Incense of the day: Jasmine

A Lemon Cleansing Spell

At this time of year, negative energy can build up in our homes. To clear away any bad vibrations, try this simple spell.

You'll need a lemon and some black pepper. Slice the lemon in half and dip each cut side in some pepper. Place the lemon halves in opposite corners of a room or in opposite corners of your home. As you set each lemon half in a corner, say:

Lemon cleanse, pepper sting.

*Surround this home with a
protective ring.*

Leave the lemon halves in place for twenty-four hours, then discard. If the lemon turns dark in that short amount of time, you may want to do this spell again, because you might have some really negative energy hanging around. If your space is very large, use more than one lemon.

James Kambos

February 5
Friday

4th ♑

Color of the day: Purple
Incense of the day: Violet

Forgive Your Heart

We've all had a bad relationship, whether with a lover, friend, family member, or coworker. These relationships leave us with negative feelings, like anger, resentment, and guilt. We might not be able to heal the relationship, but we can heal ourselves. Forgiving ourselves for these negative feelings is necessary for us to move on.

Write down on a piece of paper all of the negative feelings you have regarding a particular relationship. Don't be afraid to admit them to yourself. This can sometimes be the hardest aspect of moving on—admitting what you are capable of.

Roll up the piece of paper and tie it closed with a black ribbon. Place it into a fireproof container and set it on fire.

As the paper burns, say:

These feelings have taken over,

Making my heart heavy and sad.

Burn them away,

Remove them,

And cleanse my heart and soul.

Allow my heart to forgive and heal.

This is my wish,

So mote it be.

Repeat this chant for as long as you feel is necessary.

Kerri Connor

NOTES:

4th ♑

☽ v/c 10:54 am

Color of the day: Brown
Incense of the day: Magnolia

Body Blessings

Rastafarians believe that the body is a temple. In honor of Bob Marley, musician and Rasta born this day in 1945, invoke a piece of Rastafarian wisdom by consecrating your body as a sacred space.

Bathe and dress yourself in clean, comfortable clothing, then stand in front of a mirror. Gaze into your own eyes, visualizing them as windows in the temple that houses your soul. Using an unprocessed, natural oil such as olive, coconut, sunflower, or hemp, anoint your forehead, heart, the palm of each hand, and your belly and feet, then chant a mantra inspired by Marley's song:

I love myself. I love my life.

For as long as you can afterward, consume unprocessed, natural foods, drink water, and get enough rest—in other words, clean and refresh your temple. Repeat frequently to love yourself and your life.

Natalie Zaman

February 7
Sunday

4th ♑

☽ → ♒ 12:59 am

Color of the day: Yellow
Incense of the day: Frankincense

Brave New Life

Deep in the earth is the eternal stirring. In the darkness of soil, a brave quickening begins. We're still in the deep clutches of winter, but it's time to plant seeds of new life.

Take a sheet of paper and a pen. Cast a circle, and in sacred space ask:

What newness do I welcome?
What seeds do I plant?
What new life shall I grow?

Let dreams, wishes, and inspiration for the coming "sprouting" be heard and recorded. Now fold the paper in quarters, thanking the directions and opening sacred space. Place the paper in an empty can and go outdoors. Hold the can in mitten-covered hands, light the paper on fire, and walk—down the block, lane, or steps. Say:

Smoke, take my newness and plant these seeds. Fertility, creativity, and new life come to me.

Dallas Jennifer Cobb

 # February 8
Monday

4th ♒

☽ v/c 9:39 am

New Moon 9:39 am

Color of the day: Silver
Incense of the day: Neroli

Chinese New Year (Monkey)

Year of the Fire Monkey

Gong hey fat choy, and welcome to the Year of the Fire Monkey! Today and in the coming weeks, as we transition from the gently industrious Wood Sheep cycle into the boldly motivated Fire Monkey cycle, see if you notice that the energy is comparable to a manicured garden exploding into a supercharged fireworks display. You may feel as though you've been working behind the scenes and humbly moving toward your goals, and now it's time to be outrageous and bold as you step confidently into the floodlights and bask in your success. To celebrate this shift and align yourself with the uniquely auspicious wave of energy that arrives today, build a fire in a fireplace or fire pit, or simply light a number of bright red and orange candles on your altar. Stand before the fire (or candles) and feel/envision yourself being filled, cleansed, enlivened, and empowered by the crackling flames.

Tess Whitehurst

February 9
Tuesday

1st ≈

☽ → ♓ 3:31 am

Color of the day: Maroon
Incense of the day: Cinnamon

Mardi Gras (Fat Tuesday)

Mardi Gras

Today is known worldwide as a holiday of decadence and feasting just prior to the Christian period of Lent. We Pagans can also think about these energies and have our own "fat Tuesday" prior to a period of abstinence of some sort. This year, consider what you might be willing to give up—if only to learn what it would be like to give up something important to you. Write down your best idea. Then feast and party, enjoying your indulgences! When you wake in the morning, complete the spell by writing down how long your "fast from ____" will last. Read the paper aloud at your altar in the form of a positive statement ("I will" rather than "I won't"). In the days to come, keep the paper with the written statement at your altar where you can see it, to remind you of your goal.

Thuri Calafia

February 10
Wednesday

1st ♓

☽ v/c 11:25 pm

Color of the day: Yellow
Incense of the day: Honeysuckle

Ash Wednesday

Empowering Yourself Through Nature

Sometimes we get so wrapped up in our everyday existence that we lose our connection to the natural world. To help stay connected, we can practice recycling, gardening, animal raising, and local food consumption. We can also choose to stay abreast of both global and local environmental issues, and even choose to practice environmental activism and education.

To renew your connection to nature, take an apple and a stick of your favorite incense to a forest or park. Find the tree that calls to you. Light the incense (safely), then in gratitude to the dryad (the spirit of the tree), offer the apple in a nook of the tree so that it can be consumed by the forces of nature, both seen and unseen. Sit beneath the tree with your back against the trunk. Enter a meditative state of consciousness, and envision the essence of the tree and the earth merging with your aura.

After you've swapped energy with the element of earth, extinguish the incense and leave it at the base of the tree. Declare:

*Nature within and nature without,
guide my life as I serve you throughout.*
Raven Digitalis

NOTES:

February 11

Thursday

1st ♓

☽ → ♈ 4:55 am

Color of the day: Green
Incense of the day: Clove

Blessing Your Books

A lot of Witches and Pagans are book lovers. I know I have lots of books that hold strong senti-mental value and useful information that I would never want to lose. For our own books of shadows, a book blessing is often used, and one of the functions of this blessing is to act as a protection. We can also use this concept to protect all our other important books.

To work this spell, you can either hold a single book in your hands or stand in front of a bookshelf with your palms facing it. Visualize white light streaming from your hands into the book(s), forming a web of energy around it/them. To seal the spell, say:

Tome(s) of knowledge, wisdom's form,

I shield you from theft and harm.

Blessing and protection,
forever encased,

Protecting my book(s) from
dangers faced.

Michael Furie

 February 12

Friday

1st ♈

Color of the day: White
Incense of the day: Cypress

Blessing of Beauty

The world around us is full of beauty, from the majesty of the natural world to the grace of a friend's laughter. Sadly, it can some-times be very difficult to see that beauty. When you're in need of a boost in your ability to appreciate the beauty around you, speak the following blessing:

May the blessing of beauty be upon me this day.

Bright radiance, help me to release pessimism and cynicism.

Comforting love, lift the weight of lead from my soul.

Majestic nature, help me to appreciate the good that surrounds me.

Gentle beauty, help me to see as you see.

Emily Carlin

February 13

Saturday

1st ♈

☽ v/c 5:32 am

☽ → ♉ 6:36 am

Color of the day: Gray
Incense of the day: Rue

Remembrance at Parentalia

Parentalia was an ancient Roman festival that began on February 13. It was a time to celebrate honored ancestors. You can honor your beloved family members on this day by bringing flowers and wine to their graves in true Parentalia tradition. If you don't have a grave to visit, create a small altar space on a shelf, desk, or tabletop. Add photographs or some other bits of memorabilia such as collectibles, jewelry, books, or whatever makes you think of the ancestors you want to honor. Whether at the grave or the altar, offer fresh flowers and wine while thinking about all the gifts that your ancestor passed on to you, and feel their spirit flowing through your blood, living in your DNA. As you focus on these gifts, give thanks:

Here I am, you live within me.

I honor you and your legacy.

I feel your blessings within my bones.

I thank you deeply across the unknown.

Mickie Mueller

 February 14

Sunday

1st ♉

Color of the day: Orange
Incense of the day: Juniper

Valentine's Day

Valentine's Rose Spell

Valentine's Day provides an opportunity to celebrate romantic love, surely, but whether we are romantically involved with someone or not, we shouldn't lose sight of the fact that the holiday is an opportunity to celebrate all forms of love   including self-appreciation and self-acceptance. It is important to love and take care of ourselves, for if we do not nurture ourselves, we cannot fully offer our best self to anyone else.

Today, acquire a pink rose and place it in a vase on your altar. Pink roses are often associated with appreciation and gratitude. On a piece of paper, write down five things you are proud of and admire about yourself. Phrase each one in the second person ("You are…"). Stand before your altar, look into a small mirror, and recite the list to yourself. Then place the list in front of the rose in the vase. Whenever you are feeling down on yourself, review this list.

Blake Octavian Blair

February 15

Monday

1st ♉

2nd Quarter 2:46 am

☽ v/c 5:54 am

☽ → ♊ 9:35 am

Color of the day: Gray
Incense of the day: Clary sage

Presidents' Day (observed)

Cross-Dressing as a Magickal Act

Magickal folk are known for being a bit out of the ordinary. Because we often channel the space between the worlds, we can easily perform certain ritualistic acts that merge the space between "this" and "that."

Cross-dressing is an ancient and multicultural practice that helps merge social paradigms of masculinity and femininity. The gender spectrum is rich rather than binary, and numerous gender expressions exist. Contemplate your idea of "male" and "female." If you personally identify with either of these social gender titles, try dressing in clothing that you feel socially represents the "opposite" gender. Perform a ritual (whether a sabbat, an esbat, or a personal working) where you summon and honor the God and Goddess equally. During the ritual, declare your adherence to the mystical arts by boldly displaying yourself as a walker between worlds. Think about what gender roles mean to you, and how you can bend these social standards in your daily existence.

Raven Digitalis

Notes:

February 16
Tuesday

2nd ♊

Color of the day: Red
Incense of the day: Ginger

Going to Battle

When you have exhausted all other options, sometimes putting on the battle armor to go to war is the only option. If you have been faced with a situation at work—be it harassment or discrimination—and you need to go to the next level, you will want to make sure you are prepared.

Today, you can tap into the Mars energies to help you when you decide to confront the issue. Visualize yourself in a solid suit of armor. This suit completely surrounds and protects you and will continue to do so when you take the issue up with your supervisor or human resources. Mars will lend you his battle readiness and keep you level-headed. When you are ready, you can call on him for added protection and strength:

Mars, lend to me a clear and battle-ready head, free of emotion and doubt. Keep me grounded and ready.

Charlynn Walls

February 17
Wednesday

2nd ♊

☽ v/c 11:37 am

☽ → ♋ 2:24 pm

Color of the day: Topaz
Incense of the day: Marjoram

Feral Cat Protection Spell

As we make our way through the depths of winter, let's not forget our furry friends who may be struggling in the cold. Feral cats are vulnerable to the elements, cars, and local wildlife. When you can, offer them practical aid such as food or shelter, but also offer a spell of protection to help them survive and thrive during this challenging time.

Draw the outline of a cat or a cat's head on the pavement outside your home in chalk. Don't worry about making a perfect drawing. As you work, recite this incantation for protection:

Food for your belly, warmth for your bones,

Shelter from the storm—or perhaps, a home.

Find comfort and joy, feral, furry friend,

Until the winter comes to an end.

And ever after.

Repeat the protection charm throughout the winter months.

Natalie Zaman

February 18
Thursday

2nd ♋

Color of the day: White
Incense of the day: Nutmeg

Spell for Abundance

Winter is a great time to examine our finances and make plans for increasing prosperity. But it's also a good time to think about our true needs versus our wants and to clarify what "abundance" means to us.

For this spell, gather three personal items: one you absolutely need, one you like but don't necessarily need, and one that is not useful or necessary at all. Place them side by side in front of you. Take up the first one and say:

I am blessed to have all that I need.

Put it down, and pick up the second item, and say:

I am capable of working for the things I desire.

Put down the second item and pick up the third, saying:

I can let go of what does not serve me.

Look at all three items and say:

I have an abundance of riches in my life.

Give the third item to charity or a friend. Do this spell once a month to help you purge unnecessary belongings, to give positive reinforcement to your efforts to build prosperity, and to clarify what you need and want in your life.

Peg Aloi

NOTES:

February 19

Friday

2nd ♋

☉ → ♓ 12:34 am

☽ v/c 9:36 am

☽ → ♌ 9:17 pm

Color of the day: Coral
Incense of the day: Orchid

Cut It Out Spell

Perform this spell to "cut out" a bad situation, problem, or habit from your life. You'll need about three feet of natural jute garden twine and a pair of scissors. Think of no more than three things you want to remove from your life. Hold the twine and say:

> I want to cut (say the problem) from my life.

Then cut a section of twine with the scissors and set it aside. You may repeat this procedure two more times for other problems if you wish. When done, pick up the pieces of twine and squeeze them in your hands. Grip them as if you're angry. Then take the twine outside and lay the pieces over the branch of a tree or shrub, but don't tie them. Hopefully birds will use the twine for nest material soon, and in doing so, your problems will be carried away.

James Kambos

 February 20

Saturday

2nd ♌

Color of the day: Blue
Incense of the day: Sage

To Grow Closer to Someone

So, Valentine's Day didn't bring you all you dreamed it would. There's still hope, though. This simple spell will help you to grow closer to your partner—provided that he or she is interested in you and just needs a bit more persuading!

You'll need two small pieces of rose-quartz crystal. Place one stone at each end of a bookshelf or windowsill, and every morning move the crystals about a quarter inch closer to each other. As you do, say:

> We grow closer together.

This is a very simple but effective way of bridging the gap between you and your partner. Remember, though, that this does not take away another person's free will. It's simply helping to deepen the connection that is already blooming between the two of you.

Charlie Rainbow Wolf

February 21

Sunday

2nd ♌

☽ v/c 8:17 pm

Color of the day: Amber
Incense of the day: Eucalyptus

Amethyst Spell for Psychic Ability and Awareness

The gorgeous amethyst stone encourages psychic ability and awareness. Many people are uneasy with psychic experiences. This amethyst spell is designed to help you learn to roll with your psychic talents and not fight against them.

You may work this spell with small amethyst points, tumbled stones, or amethyst jewelry. Hold the crystal or jewelry in your hands and repeat this spell:

The amethyst does promote psychic ability,

In this waxing-moon phase, please grant awareness to me.

Psychic experiences I will accept with grace.

My visions and premonitions I will now embrace.

Whether I can psychically see, hear, know, or feel,

My awareness is heightened, and I'm ready to deal.

By all the power of the waxing moon so bright,

I conjure to increase my awareness tonight.

Now pocket the stone or wear the jewelry, and embrace your psychic talents!

Ellen Dugan

Notes:

February 22
Monday

2nd ♌

☽ → ♍ 6:24 am

Full Moon 1:20 pm

Color of the day: Ivory
Incense of the day: Narcissus

Mindfulness Tea Meditation

We all have times when we feel anxious or stressed, as if our minds are too full to think clearly. We can use the simple, everyday ritual of making and enjoying a cup of tea to help us relax and restore balance.

First choose an appropriate tea. You might choose a bright, astringent green tea to help with clarity of thought, a strong black to help stabilize your energy levels, or a gentle herbal blend for releasing negative energy. This is a great time to treat yourself to the highest-quality tea you have.

As you prepare the tea, take a moment to think of the energy you wish to release. Let the aroma of the brewing tea flow into your body and loosen any tight muscles. Allow the negative energy to ground.

Take time and really enjoy your tea as you drink it. Let the energy of the tea flow into you. Let each sip fill you with calm and balance.

Emily Carlin

February 23
Tuesday

3rd ♍

Color of the day: Black
Incense of the day: Bayberry

Blessing Boundaries and Borders

In the ancient Roman culture, Terminalia was celebrated on this date, honoring the god Terminus, who ruled over boundaries and frontiers. Romans would pour libations on their stone boundary-markers to infuse them with magical energy for protection. They knew that healthy boundaries made for healthy relationships, and good fences made for great neighbors.

Whether you live in an urban apartment, in a village house, on a rural farm, or in shared community space, determine what the boundary-markers are for your space, and infuse them with magical energy. Choose the appropriate libation: wine or ale, juice, or steeped herbal tea. Pour it into a glass or cup infused with your personal energy. Walk your boundary lines, stopping frequently to pour a few drops of liquid libation, incanting:

Terminus, be with me and protect this space.

Establish good boundaries, good borders, good neighbors, and always a safe place.

Dallas Jennifer Cobb

February 24
Wednesday

3rd ♏

☽ v/c 9:22 am

☽ → ♎ 5:41 pm

Color of the day: Brown
Incense of the day: Bay laurel

Money Bags

The holidays are over and bills are coming due. For many businesses, this is the slowest time of year, and employees often find their hours have been cut, making it a tight squeeze financially. Use this spell to help keep the money flowing in during this time.

You will need a rectangle of green material about 4 x 2 inches in size, plus a needle, thread, and oak moss. You don't need to be an expert seamstress for this. Fold the material in half, with the outside on the inside, making a square, and sew 2½ sides shut. Turn it inside out, stuff with oak moss, and sew shut.

At your altar, bless the square and sprinkle a few drops of whiskey or other hard liquor on it (or use moon water) to charge it and as an offering to your deities. Keep the square with you at all times, either wearing it next to your skin (preferred) or carrying it in your pocket.

Kerri Connor

February 25
Thursday

3rd ♎

Color of the day: Purple
Incense of the day: Myrrh

Build a Prosperity Altar

Sometimes it can be difficult to keep prosperity cycling into our lives. To ensure that you're creating a positive, healthy relationship with the money you need to care for yourself and loved ones, create a prosperity altar.

Clear off a shelf, a corner of a dresser, or a section of a bookshelf for your altar. Include items such as acorns, your favorite prosperity deity, a dish of rice or salt, coins, cinnamon sticks, raw emerald, aventurine, tiger's-eye, a gold candle holder, an incense burner, and natural representations of the four elements. Keep green and gold candles handy for quick spells, and a beautiful dish where you can drop coins from time to time to keep the energy of prosperity flowing. Here is a charm to dedicate your prosperity altar:

I dedicate this altar fair,

By fire, water, earth, and air.

Money is energy that we all need.

Here it flows forth and comes to me!

Mickie Mueller

February 26

Friday

3rd ♎

☽ v/c 6:18 am

Color of the day: Rose
Incense of the day: Alder

Weaving Blessings of Friendship

Fridays are rife with the energy of love in all its forms, including that of friendship. Handmade gifts charged with love and gratitude are a wonderful way to show somebody how much you care. Today, make simple friendship bracelets for you and a friend. There are many free patterns readily available online. The knotting and weaving process involved in the bracelets' creation is perfect for focusing your intent and weaving blessings and energy into the creation. As you knot and weave, focus on chanting the following:

As I weave, I bless you.

*True friends we are, through
and through.*

Gratitude and love, I give to you.

May all the love and support you give

Return abundantly to you.

Use the same chant for both bracelets, as learning to love and accept yourself and striving to be a good friend to others in return are important goals as well.

Blake Octavian Blair

February 27

Saturday

3rd ♎

☽ → ♏ 6:26 am

Color of the day: Black
Incense of the day: Pine

Polar Bear Vision Quest

It's International Polar Bear Day. In addition to the polar bear's inherent worth as a sacred sibling on our beloved planet, s/he also possesses great magical worth as a totem and guide on both the physical and spiritual planes. Symbolizing transformation and survival, this grand white bear's most quintessential medicine is the ability to usher us from one phase or quality of life to another. Polar bears are seen as psychopomps (who guide us to the otherworld after death) as well as initiators into new levels of perception and power.

Today, light a white candle, play entrancing instrumental music, and take a vision quest through a snowy landscape to meet the polar bear. Offer a gift, and be open to receiving any guidance or blessings you may be offered. Say thank you and return. Afterward, find a charity that supports polar bears and donate any amount that you can comfortably afford (even a dollar!).

Tess Whitehurst

February 28
Sunday

3rd ♏

Color of the day: Orange
Incense of the day: Heliotrope

Taking Stock

Today's waning gibbous moon has good energy for shining a light on all that we still have to do to prepare for spring and planting time, whether in a backyard garden or a more private, inner landscape.

Take a few stones and paint them with runes or other symbols that have meaning to you personally. Then fill a plant pot or small dish with soil or sand. "Plant" the painted stones in the top layer of soil/sand, face down for divination, leaving a space in the middle for your candle. In a meditative space, carve a white candle with messages of all you wish to harvest this year. "Plant" the candle in the pot or dish filled with soil/sand and stones. Light the candle, saying:

> What needs to be cleared to make way for this harvest?

After the candle has burned all the way down, carefully remove it. See if the wax melted onto any of the stones, and read the patterns there. You can also perform a divination by simply pulling a few of the stones you painted, and interpreting their meaning. May all your gardens be blessed!

Thuri Calafia

February 29
Monday

3rd ♏

☽ v/c 2:55 pm

☽ → ♐ 6:56 pm

Color of the day: White
Incense of the day: Hyssop

Leap Day Wish Spell

The lore surrounding this day often relates to shifting an established paradigm. Much like a sabbat, leap day can be seen as outside of normal time and brimming with potential. Since the energy attached to the day is one of upending current patterns, it lends itself well to spells designed to change something completely—e.g., transforming bad luck to good, or illness to health, etc., as opposed to increasing or decreasing an already established structure.

To cast this spell, write your desire on a piece of paper and burn an incense of equal parts myrrh and frankincense in a cauldron. Charge the paper with your intent and say:

> Transform the bad into good,
>
> Outside of time; bright new day.
>
> Shift in fortune now ensured,
>
> A fresh new start comes my way.

Speak your specific wish three times, then carefully ignite the paper in the candle's flame, dropping it into the cauldron.

Michael Furie

March

March is a time of changes and a time of changelings, a time of starts and stops and renewal. This month often begins in one season and ends in another. Other months bring transitions, but March may very well bring the most radical changes. Many a blizzard has halted the commerce of a region one week of March, while sunshine and green grass and flowers overrun the week before or after.

This month being named for Mars, the god of war, means protection of self and home also figures large at this time. Ancient calendars focus on March as the start of the new year. More recently, the 15th, or the "Ides of March," brought ill fortune to Julius Caesar, and is considered by many to be unlucky. The last three days of March, long thought to be "borrowed days" of April, also call for caution. Consider doing just a little more to guard against negative energy of any sort, especially from the 10th to the 31st. A thorough house-cleaning may be in order.

In the middle of that period of caution we celebrate the vernal equinox. Ostara—the Eastern Star—is the spoke of the Wheel of the Year observed in March for earth-based believers. Paint and hide the eggs, honor the Lady with symbols of rabbits, and create your own revelry.

Emyme

March 1

Tuesday

3rd ♐

4th Quarter 6:11 pm

Color of the day: Maroon
Incense of the day: Cinnamon

This Little Pig...

Pigs are resourceful, intelligent, self-reliant, and fearless creatures. As a totem animal, they invoke wealth, prosperity, and luck. Take today—National Pig Day in the United States—to work some porcine magic.

Cut five 9-inch lengths of pink ribbon. One at a time, starting with your thumb and ending with your pinky finger, wrap a strand around each digit of one hand so that it resembles a pig's curly tail. As you wind, revise an old rhyme to invoke pig energy:

This little pig is lucky,

This little pig is smart.

This little pig has all that he needs,

And this little pig has heart.

And this little pig imparts to me—
everything a pig should be!

Unwind the ribbons from your fingers, then tie them together and carry them as a charm for luck and prosperity.

Natalie Zaman

 March 2

Wednesday

4th ♐

☽ v/c 9:55 pm

Color of the day: Topaz
Incense of the day: Lavender

Electronic Purge

Because we use our computers as everything from calendars to navigators to primary communication devices, clearing electronic clutter from a computer or phone can actually have quite magical benefits, such as a clearer mind, more desirable opportunities, more stress-free travel, and swifter and more harmonious communications.

Today, the conditions are ideal for an electronic purge. Carve the symbol for Mercury (☿) into a white candle, and surround the candle with a circle of salt on a plate or candle holder. Light the candle and then purge away. Delete old e-mails, photos you don't want, and apps you no longer need. You might even refresh your screen saver with an uplifting nature photo or a vision board collage. Even if you only have ten minutes, set a timer and clear! When you're finished, affirm:

I am in divine flow. My communications are blessed. I welcome blessings and opportunities in abundance.

Tess Whitehurst

March 3
Thursday

4th ♐

☽ → ♑ 5:01 am

Color of the day: Crimson
Incense of the day: Carnation

Blessing a Cellphone for Protection

To a lot of people, myself included, our cellphones are practically a part of us. The idea of losing our phone is unthinkable! Aside from having insurance and keeping careful track of our phone, we also have magical options at our disposal to keep it safe from theft or our own forgetfulness. The very notion takes the term "charging your cellphone" to a new place.

Hold the phone in your hands and envision a glowing orb of white light. See this light condensing to form a shell around the phone. To focus the intent, say this spell:

Window to the world, contact link,

Protected from theft and loss;

I charge you now to be free from harm,

Damage rejected and pilfering blocked.

Keep the phone on your person for the rest of the day.

Michael Furie

March 4
Friday

4th ♑

Color of the day: Coral
Incense of the day: Vanilla

Inspiration for Accomplishment

On this day in 1933, as part of the start of the Roosevelt administration, Frances Perkins became the first woman to serve in the U.S. cabinet. Perkins's accomplishment reminds us that we all possess the potential to achieve great things in life.

Think of a large goal you desire to achieve, and gather an orange or gold candle (colors associated with success) and a safe holder. Carve a symbol, a few words, or a phrase representing your goal into the candle. Hold the candle between your hands and up to your third-eye chakra, and visualize yourself accomplishing your goal. Then light the candle and supervise it until it safely burns out on its own, snuffing and relighting as necessary until it has burned all the way down. As the candle burns, know that your intentions are being sent into the universe. So mote it be!

Blake Octavian Blair

March 5
Saturday

4th ℞

☽ v/c 11:05 am

☽ → ♒ 11:22 am

Color of the day: Indigo

Incense of the day: Rue

Good Riddance Spell

Okay, you've just been dumped. Don't waste time getting even with the person (that creates bad karma). Instead, get over your ex with this spell. Gather these ingredients:

- A piece of black or purple fabric
- A pinch each of lavender, sage, and black tea
- Black thread

On the fabric, blend together the herbs and tea. Stir them in a counterclockwise direction. Draw the corners of the fabric up and tie with the thread. Next turn the water on full force in the bathroom sink or bathtub. Hold the pouch to your heart and say:

Water, cleanse away my hurt and pain.
He/She will never hurt me again.

Untie your pouch and toss your herbs/tea into the running water. Turn off the water and let the mixture swirl down the drain—taking your hurt with it.

James Kambos

March 6
Sunday

4th ♒

Color of the day: Gold

Incense of the day: Frankincense

Cutting Ties

This Crone's sickle moon is a good time to see what ties need to be cut in your life. Perhaps there's a project you need to set aside or reassign, or a relationship that's not working. Ponder all the ties you have to your energy and resources, and then write down each one on a piece of cardstock or paper in an appropriate color (for example, blue for an emotional tie). Thread some black string through the card, and tie the other end to a black string you've tied around your waist.

Ground and center. Twirl deosil, letting the corded cards flutter around you. As you do so, say, nine times:

I'm spinning with all these responsibilities! I now KNOW which ones to cut!

At the end of your chant, slow to a stop and turn widdershins as you cut the lines you need to sever, saying:

I let you go in grace and love.
Be blessed.

Burn the cords and the discards, as well as any guilt you feel.

Thuri Calafia

March 7
Monday

4th ♒︎

☽ v/c 3:46 am

☽ → ♓︎ 2:08 pm

Color of the day: Gray
Incense of the day: Lily

Clearing Your Tarot Deck or Divination Tool

It's easy to take for granted the fact that our divination tools need regular cleansing and clearing. Keeping in mind that these tools are the hosts of both cosmic and interpersonal energies, it only makes sense that their essence needs to be realigned every now and again.

Enter a sacred space and "work" the tool(s). Shuffle the cards, riffle through the runes, roll the crystal ball—whatever you need to do.

Approach the east and bless the tool(s) with the smoke of sage.

Approach the south and bless the tool(s) with the flame of a candle.

Approach the west and bless the tool(s) with pure and sacred water.

Approach the north and bless the tool(s) with a hefty amount of salt.

Finally, set the tool(s) in a windowsill to soak up both sunlight and moonlight for however many days your intuition guides you to do so. Happy divining!

Raven Digitalis

March 8
Tuesday

4th ♓︎

☽ v/c 8:54 pm

New Moon 8:54 pm

Color of the day: White
Incense of the day: Geranium

Solar Eclipse

A New Moon Spell for Love, Joy, and Abundance

This is an excellent spell to perform under a new moon, because a starry night is best for this. Don't worry about cloud cover—it's the intent that is the magic, not the weather.

You'll need an orange, a drinking glass, a piece of paper, and a pen. After dark, cut the orange in half and squeeze the juice into the glass. On the piece of paper, write what you want to come true. Fold the paper three times. Drink the orange juice. Fold the paper another three times. Now bury the paper outside, with the orange peels. Do this in the dark of the night, while the stars are still shining.

You can now stop wishing for what you want to happen, and start to work toward it. The spell is cast, and you're on your way to manifesting your wish.

Charlie Rainbow Wolf

March 9
Wednesday

1st ♓

☽ → ♈ 2:40 pm

Color of the day: Brown
Incense of the day: Lilac

Fairy Circles

When a fairy circle pops up overnight in your yard, you know that the fae are watching you and your home. Be a kind neighbor and show respect, and they will help you in your magickal endeavors. Leave offerings nearby or inside of the fairy ring. Include items like coins, mead, cheese, and bread as your tokens. Be sure to leave the offerings regularly so they do not feel slighted.

Once you have established a rapport with your new neighbors, you can see if they will assist you. When petitioning the fae for their help, write your request on a slip of paper and leave it inside the ring. Be careful not to disturb the ring while you do so. Using a small rock to keep the paper from blowing away is a good idea.

Charlynn Walls

March 10
Thursday

1st ♈

Color of the day: Purple
Incense of the day: Jasmine

Prosperity Spell with Clover

Today we have a waxing moon phase and it's a Jupiter day—perfect for prosperity magick! For this spell, let's work with clover. Yes, that's the clover found in the lawn. Go pick a few stems and get ready to cast. Hold the clover in your hands and visualize its natural magick seeping right into your palms. Picture prosperity coming to you in the best way possible. Now say this charm:

Magickal clover, full of prosperity and power,

I conjure you to assist me in this hour.

Add your natural magick gently to mine,

Bring wealth and success at the sound of my rhyme.

By waxing moon, my prosperity will increase,

A positive change will my magick now release!

Keep the clover stems in your wallet until after the next full moon, then return them to nature.

Ellen Dugan

March 11
Friday

1st ♈

☽ v/c 1:24 pm

☽ → ♉ 2:44 pm

Color of the day: Pink

Incense of the day: Mint

Spell to Increase Freelance Work

Many people are working as freelancers these days. It can be difficult to find more assignments, given recent changes in technology and communication. No wonder our confidence can slip away without us even noticing.

Try this simple spell to help generate more freelance work. Get a multicolored stack of sticky notes. On each note, write one word that reminds you of how unique and effective your work is. These might be words like "reliable," "wordsmith," "resourceful," or "passionate."

Place these notes around your workspace: above your desk, on your computer monitor, on the doorframe, on your bulletin board, on a window, etc. When you see them, say aloud, "I am reliable!" and follow up with another related statement, such as "I get the job done!" This amounts to giving yourself small, frequent pep talks. Change the location of these notes periodically to associate them with different activities (putting "resourceful" by your wastebasket may remind you to use materials more efficiently).

Peg Aloi

NOTES:

March 12
Saturday

1st ♉

Color of the day: Black
Incense of the day: Ivy

Saturday Special

Spring's coming, and soon it will be time for spring cleaning—but not yet. Today, enjoy the languorous stretch of weekend and get ready to "reset." Undertake a personal ritual of clearing to prepare you for the spring cleaning ahead.

Gather some Epsom salt, sea salt, and a favorite essential oil—clary sage, lavender, or rose are recommended. Run a hot bath, pouring one cup each of Epsom and sea salts into the running water. Cool to the perfect temperature, add eight drops of essential oil, and slip in.

Close your eyes, breathe evenly and deeply, and slip into a meditative state. Immersion in water helps to press your reset button; salts draw impurities from the body, energy field, and spirit; and essential oils anoint and restore healing, peace, and clarity.

Breathe consciously, meditating:

I exhale toxins, inhaling health.

I exhale anxiety, inhaling peace.

I exhale confusion, inhaling clarity.

With these, I reset and am ready.

Dallas Jennifer Cobb

 ## March 13
Sunday

1st ♉

☽ v/c 5:46 am

☽ → ♊ 5:03 pm

Color of the day: Amber
Incense of the day: Marigold

Daylight Saving Time begins at 2:00 am

A hastening Spell

You'll need to stay up late the night before to perform this spell! It is designed to help you lose something over a period of time.

For this effective banishing spell, you'll need three candles: one blue, one gold, and one white. At 2:00 am, light the blue candle and say:

May time whirl around me.

May speed gather in me.

Light the gold candle and say:

May I hasten to my calling.

May my tomorrow be today.

Write on a piece of paper what you want time to take from you. Light the white candle and set the paper alight safely. When it has been fully burned, set the clock forward. Pause for a moment and know that whatever was burdening you has been taken from you in the hour that has been stolen from the night. Then pinch out the gold candle, then the blue one, and finally the white one.

Dispose of the ashes somewhere off your premises. It is done.

Charlie Rainbow Wolf

NOTES:

 March 14
Monday

1st ♊

Color of the day: Lavender
Incense of the day: Neroli

Cleansing Rain

Into every life a little rain must fall, so why not use it to your magickal advantage? A spring rainstorm is an excellent time to do a self-cleansing spell.

The next time it rains, step outside into the rain and envision it washing away negativity and stagnant energy. Before you go outside, be sure you've got dry clothes and some warm tea ready for when you're done—we don't want anyone catching cold for magick's sake.

Step outside and allow the rain and wind to soak you. Recite the following words:

Blessed rain, wash away old hurts and soothe my soul.

Blessed rain, rinse away the stains and grit of time.

Blessed rain, clean away ill thoughts that leave a hole.

Blessed rain, purify all that is me and mine.

Then go back inside, dry off, and warm up.

Emily Carlin

March 15
Tuesday

1st ♊

☽ v/c 1:03 pm

2nd Quarter 1:03 pm

☽ → ♋ 8:57 pm

Color of the day: Gray

Incense of the day: Ylang-ylang

Visualize Your Life

Use today to plan out your goals, projects, conquests—anything you have coming up that you want to be successful. Use a spell journal (if you don't have one, start one!) to write down your goals, providing as much detail as possible. Include the steps you will need to take to be successful, but also include what success will look and feel like. How will this affect your life? Write about your successful end result as if it has already happened.

As you write, visualize your success as well, focusing on it as if it has already happened. Be sure to include as many details as possible in your visualization. End both your journal entry and your visualization with these words:

This is my wish, so mote it be.

Kerri Connor

March 16
Wednesday

2nd ♋

Color of the day: White

Incense of the day: Lavender

Spell to honor Bacchus and Dionysus

This day was sacred to the Roman god Bacchus and Greek god Dionysus. Both gods (and Pan, the forest god) are associated with intoxication, imagination, our "wild side," and our deeper intuitive nature.

Set up your altar with some grapes or a small goblet of wine or beer, and a crown of ivy (traditionally worn by both gods). Stand before your altar unclothed or wearing a simple robe. Play music with drums and flutes that reminds you of the forest (such as music by Deep Forest or Gabrielle Roth, or the Jethro Tull song "Pan Dance"). Put the crown of ivy on your head. Eat some grapes or sip from the goblet. Give thanks to the gods for their gifts of fruit and wine. Close your eyes and move to the music. Imagine dancing in the forest to the drums, as the ancients did. Keep the ivy crown on your altar to remind you to honor your wild side and your connection to nature.

Peg Aloi

March 17
Thursday

2nd ♋

Color of the day: Turquoise
Incense of the day: Nutmeg

Saint Patrick's Day

Lucky Peas

Many people celebrate Saint Patrick's Day on March 17, but if you're looking for some green luck magic, look no further than the humble pea! Peas bring good luck for both money and love, and the luckiest day to plant them is on March 17.

Plant some spring peas in your garden or in a container. There are many varieties to choose from, so pick one that's perfect for your planting needs. Plant your peas according to the directions on the package, then add some extra luck by mixing up some milk and honey to bless your new peas. Dip your fingertips into the milk and honey mixture and flick it lightly over the sown peas. As you do so, add this charm:

Bless my peas with milk and honey,

Whether it be love or money.

Lucky peas will grow and grow,

I will reap the luck I sow.

Mickie Mueller

March 18
Friday

2nd ♋

☽ v/c 12:09 am

☽ → ♌ 3:54 am

Color of the day: Rose
Incense of the day: Thyme

A Spell to Find a Furry (or Finned or Feathered or Scaled) Friend

Adopting a pet isn't always an easy process. Filling out applications, waiting, and then meeting potential future family members can be as tiring and frustrating as it is rewarding. To ease the process, write the name of the type of animal you want to adopt on a blank piece of paper, and place it on your altar (you can also make a general statement, such as "Let the right animal for me come to me"). Weigh the paper down with four stones: rose quartz for the love you will give and receive, smoky quartz for endurance of the adoption process, garnet for the commitment you will be making, and turquoise for the joy you will give and receive through pet ownership. As you place each stone, speak your desire aloud:

Paw, claw, fin, or feather,

I know we will find each other!

Leave the message on your altar until your new family member joins you.

Natalie Zaman

March 19
Saturday

2nd ♌

☽ v/c 4:43 pm

Color of the day: Brown
Incense of the day: Rue

Elemental Spell for Peace

The time of the equinox is wonderful for conflict resolution, the balance of the moment being harnessed to bring peace among people. An effective spell for this purpose uses ingredients aligned to each of the elements. First, make a Peace Oil from ½ cup olive oil (fire) and 1 tablespoon each of vervain (earth), lavender (air), and chamomile (water). Simmer the ingredients in a pot over very low heat until the air is fragrant. Remove from heat, allowing the mixture to cool. Once cooled, strain it and charge the oil for peace by visualizing light-blue energy and a calm feeling absorbing into the liquid.

To cast the spell, write the names of those whose conflict you wish to end on a piece of paper. Dab the corners with the oil, placing the paper beneath a light blue candle (also anointed). Visualize the people at peace, then light the candle and say:

Conflict, stress, and tension cease;

Discord melted, I call for peace.

Repeat three times.

Michael Furie

March 20
Sunday

2nd ♌

☉ → ♈ 12:30 am

☽ → ♍ 1:39 pm

Color of the day: Orange
Incense of the day: Hyacinth

Spring Equinox – Ostara –
Palm Sunday

Pendulum Board Blessing

When working with new tools, it is important to make sure they are consecrated and blessed. Doing so tunes the items to your personal energies and makes working with them easier and more natural. Today, on the spring equinox, connect to the abundant energies of the earth to bless and consecrate the pendulum and board you are using.

Take the items and place them on your altar along with the items you will consecrate the board with. Since most pendulum boards are made of wood, be cautious of what you use. To represent water, place several seashells on the board. (Water itself can damage the wood.) To represent earth, sprinkle the top with sea salt. Fire can be represented by a volcanic rock or a piece of red cloth. Finally, air can be represented by allowing incense to waft over the items. When you have placed each item on or near the board and pendulum, say:

> The power of earth, air, fire, and water do align with and consecrate the board to myself and its intended magickal purpose of divination.

Gather the items together and place in a muslin bag to store with your board.

Charlynn Walls

NOTES:

 March 21
Monday

2nd ♍

☽ v/c 11:55 pm

Color of the day: Silver
Incense of the day: Rosemary

Aquamarine Spell

Aquamarine is associated with the moon—which is perfect for today (a Monday), as it is the "moon's day"! Aquamarine can help sharpen your intuition. This is the perfect spell to enchant your aquamarine jewelry or loose stones. Hold the crystal or jewelry in your hands, and let the light of the waxing moon fall upon it. Then repeat this spell:

> By the light of tonight's waxing moon,
>
> May the moon goddess now hear this tune.
>
> Lady, empower this stone; may it sharpen my talents true,
>
> So my intuition adds clarity to all that I do.
>
> By the powers of land, sky, and sea,
>
> As I will it, then so shall it be!

Now pocket the stone or wear the jewelry, and accept your intuition for the gift that it is!

Ellen Dugan

March 22
Tuesday

2nd ♍

Color of the day: Scarlet
Incense of the day: Basil

The Journey of Sacred Objects

The Emerald Buddha, a now-iconic Buddhist statue, resided in many places before coming to rest at its current location in Wat Phra Kaew, Thailand, on this day in 1784. Sacred objects and icons often go through a long and seemingly divinely guided journey, changing hands many times until they reach their proper home and caretakers. In honor of this process and of the Emerald Buddha, today think about a sacred object in your possession that you know you are not meant to be the permanent caretaker of. Think if you know a person whom that object is meant to be passed on to, and take steps toward passing it along. Or, alternatively, think about an object you possess that is meant to be in your care but has not found its proper place in your home. Take the time today to find a place of honor in your dwelling for that sacred object.

Blake Octavian Blair

March 23
Wednesday

2nd ♍

☽ → ♎ 1:23 am

Full Moon 8:01 am

Color of the day: Yellow
Incense of the day: Marjoram

Lunar Eclipse

Full Moon Lunar Eclipse Spell

A lunar eclipse always occurs on a full moon, and it typically marks significant events in our lives, like endings or culmination points. It may even seem that your gods are determined to give you a "turbocharge" to move forward in life, to rise to your destiny, if you will. An eclipse can help get that energy moving, as it packs a bigger punch than an ordinary full moon.

If possible, perform this spell outdoors where you can see the eclipse, but indoors while it is occurring is okay, too. Ground and center, and open your arms to the Divine. Say:

I am open and willing to meet my destiny. May the signs and lessons be clear.

Then take some time to simply attune to the energies of this moon, writing down any thoughts or pictures that pop into your consciousness, especially those that seem random to you—they're telling. It's a good idea to take any messages extra seriously at this crucial time, and be blessed.

Thuri Calafia

NOTES:

 March 24
Thursday

3rd ♎

☽ v/c 4:55 pm

Color of the day: Green
Incense of the day: Apricot

Purim

Spiritual Solidarity Feast

Today happens to be both Purim and Hola Mohalla, religious holidays of communal feasting and spiritual solidarity celebrated by people of the Jewish and Sikh faiths, respectively. Additionally, it's an expansive, Jupiter-ruled Thursday, and the moon is in the loving, fair, and harmonious sign of Libra. With all of these factors in play, it's an excellent time for a "celebration of spiritual diversity" feast. Prepare or purchase a delicious vegetarian meal, and invite over one or more friends who practice a different faith or tradition than you do, letting them know your intention to celebrate your differences through the ritual sharing of a meal. Light peach and pink candles for peace and understanding. Before eating, say a solidarity prayer, such as:

For each unique person, there is a unique spiritual path. With this precious meal, we celebrate our differences while expressing our solidarity as peaceful and loving spiritual devotees. Thank you.

Tess Whitehurst

March 25
Friday

3rd ♎

☽ → ♏ 2:09 pm

Color of the day: White
Incense of the day: Cypress

Good Friday

Blessing Your Food Stocks

The fact that you're reading this book shows that you're a seeker of self-awareness. It's also likely that you have most, if not all, of your physical needs met (food, water, clothing, health, and so forth). Bearing this in mind, consider the lifestyles of other people across the globe. Bring to mind the level of abundance and wellness we have in comparison to the suffering and survival-based desperation that many people experience.

Invoke the essence of gratitude by blessing all of the food and drink you currently have on hand. Open your refrigerator, freezer, cupboards, and pantry. While you do this, examine each item thoroughly and think of its origin—where did it come from? Imagine each item glowing in a soft white light. If you wish, carry a stick of sage and smudge every edible item you own. As you do this, declare:

Abundance I receive; gratitude I give!
I enjoy and I share; I am truly blessed
to live!

Raven Digitalis

 March 26
Saturday

3rd ♏

Color of the day: Blue
Incense of the day: Sandalwood

Spell for Finishing a Writing Project

Make an anointing oil with essential oils associated with clarity: sandalwood, myrrh, rosemary, fir balsam, and/or clary sage will all work. Blend them together in a base of olive or other oil. Touch to the insides of your wrists before working or when thinking about your project. These oils will help boost your creative and verbal powers and impart clarity of thought to your process.

For some more symbolic magic, you can also rub some of the oil onto a pencil and place it next to your printed project overnight. You could also make a blend of herbs and oils into a potpourri and keep it on your altar; refresh with a few drops of essential oil when the scent fades. This will keep your thoughts and energy focused on your work.

Peg Aloi

March 27
Sunday

3rd ♏

☽ v/c 3:25 am

Color of the day: Yellow
Incense of the day: Almond

Easter

Rebirth and Renewal

Known by many as a day of rebirth, today is an ideal day to clear away old, stagnant energy and renew your soul with refreshed positive energy. Add two drops each of lemon, peppermint, frankincense, and lavender oils to a warm bath. Submerge yourself in the tub and plan on meditating for at least twenty minutes. As you soak in the tub, visualize the water washing through you. See it washing away any dirty, dingy areas of energy and replacing those areas with a crisp, bright white light. Deeply breathe in the scent. Feel it fill your lungs with that same white light. Visualize the white light pouring into your blood and then flowing throughout your arteries and veins. Chant either out loud or to yourself:

I am reborn.

I am refreshed.

I am renewed.

Kerri Connor

March 28
Monday

3rd ♏

☽ → ♐ 2:46 am

Color of the day: White
Incense of the day: Hyssop

Eggshell Spell

Eggshells have been used for ages to absorb and remove illnesses, curses, and negative energy of all kinds. Break a small hole in the top and bottom of an egg, then insert a toothpick to break up the yolk. Hold the egg over a bowl, seal your mouth over one end, blow the egg out of the shell, and then rinse the shell. Next, write all the things you want to release from your life on a small slip of paper, then roll it up and put it inside the hollow eggshell. Light a fire in your barbeque or fireplace. Hold the eggshell in your hands, and think about what you wrote on that slip of paper. Allow yourself to release everything that you want gone into the eggshell. Once you feel all has been released, toss the egg into the fire and watch as it burns up all the negativity trapped inside.

Mickie Mueller

March 29
Tuesday

3rd ♐

☽ v/c 9:55 pm

Color of the day: Black
Incense of the day: Ginger

Plant a Seed Spell

In rural areas, fields are being plowed and planting will begin soon. Take time now to plant your own "seed" for prosperity. You'll need a piece of paper, a green ink pen, a rock, potting soil, and a small flowerpot. Write your wish for abundance on the paper, then place the rock on top of your written charm. Wrap the paper around the rock, and place this bundle in the flowerpot. Cover with potting soil. Visualize your wish coming true. Place the pot in an out-of-the-way place, like a closet, and try not to think about it. When your wish comes true, bury the paper and soil outside; place the rock on your altar to remind you of the abundance Mother Earth has blessed you with. When you think it's appropriate, return the rock to the earth.

James Kambos

March 30
Wednesday

3rd ♐

☽ → ♑ 1:45 pm

Color of the day: White
Incense of the day: Honeysuckle

Blessing for Electronics

From desktops and laptops to smartphones and tablets, electronics are a major part of life for just about everyone these days. Despite their position in our lives, we rarely think to include these vital devices in our magickal protections.

For this spell, you'll need a no-scratch cleaning cloth (microfiber is best) and some protective incense (sage or dragon's blood both work well).

First, thoroughly clean the device with the cloth. Wipe away any smudges on the screen, dust from vents, etc. As you do so, envision any negative energy clinging to the device being wiped away with the grime. Then waft the incense smoke over the device and say:

Blessed be this [name of device]. May it be protected from bugs, viruses, and hackers; from water and power surges; from slips and spills; and from any ill intent. So mote it be.

Emily Carlin

March 31
Thursday

3rd ♑
4th Quarter 11:17 am

Color of the day: Crimson
Incense of the day: Myrrh

Ever Changing

In ancient Rome, the annual Feast of Luna was held today, celebrating the goddess of the moon and lunar magic. At moonrise, sit quietly in a sacred (and safe) place to invoke Luna. Draw a clockwise circle around you with the index finger of your right hand, calling in the directions:

> I invoke Luna, the divine feminine, she who rules the measurement of time, fertility cycles, calendars, and crops. Bless me with the wisdom of the moon: magic, intuition, and the eternal cycle of dark, wax, full, wane, and void. With the knowledge of the cycles of the universe, I easily ebb, flow, and change. Luna, bless me throughout every stage.

Breathe deeply. Connect to the moon, to Luna and her eternal, cyclical magic. Know that her cycle of change guides you. Close the circle with your left hand, circling counterclockwise, releasing the directions and closing sacred space.

Dallas Jennifer Cobb

NOTES:

April

April is truly the deliciousness and glory of spring! In most regions, early flowers begin showing their colors as skies clear and many birds return to their homes. Humans begin spring cleanings, and everywhere, red-blooded creatures begin pairing off for the sacred dance of courtship, whether those pairings last for a lifetime or simply a few hours. This is the month of the Sacred Marriage of the Lord and the Lady, for Beltane, or May Eve, occurs at the very end of the month, on April 30th (in some traditions, it's May 1st), and Pagans everywhere begin to plan romantic and sexy activities, from private rituals involving Great Rites to large public rituals with May gads or a Maypole. Everywhere, we see couplings, new growth, fertility, and eventually, beautiful babies of all kinds.

What will you plan for your spring celebrations? Will there be May wine? It's easy to make—just throw a handful of sweet woodruff and sliced strawberries into a punch bowl with some good white wine or champagne, and let stand for the duration of your ritual. Will you plan a Maypole dance? How about a Great Rite? Whatever you choose, do it with flair and with color, and you will be honoring the glory of spring!

Thuri Calafia

April 1
Friday

4th ♑

☽ v/c 12:39 pm

☽ → ♒ 9:37 pm

Color of the day: Pink
Incense of the day: Mint

April Fools' Day –
All Fools' Day (Pagan)

A Syllabub Spell

Word or treat, "syllabub" captures the carefree spirit of April Fools'. The world can be a stressful place, and we often forget the importance of play. Prepare a foolish dessert and infuse it (literally!) with a magical charm for fun.

Combine four parts whipped cream and one part crushed fruit (strawberries are good at this time of year). Fold the berries into the cream, being careful not to incorporate them completely. You might also want to include a ribbon of chocolate syrup. As you work, say this spell in limerick form—the most foolish kind of verse:

Eating this Fool will ensure

A happiness that will endure

Past April the first

And cannot be reversed.

Of this I am certainly sure.

Eat and share this Fools' fool to balance stress with peace and work with play—and be merry! Laughter is the best medicine and the best magic.

Natalie Zaman

NOTES:

April 2

Saturday

4℞ ≈

Color of the day: Gray
Incense of the day: Pine

Magickal Movie Night

Tally's Electric Theatre, the first motion picture theater in Los Angeles, California, opened on this day in 1902. In honor of both movie magic and Craft magick, it's time for a magickal movie night! Have a magickal friend or two over tonight, and have a viewing of your favorite movie with magickal themes and characters. Don't forget the snacks and treats—ask each guest to bring their favorite. Afterward, have a discussion of the lessons to be learned from the movie's story and how accurate or inaccurate it was to real-life Craft magick. Sometimes movies feature magick that is pleasantly realistic to that which we practice in real life—even if it does take artistic liberties and add a little cinematic sparkle around the edges. Other times the magick featured in movies is nothing like that of real-life Witches. Either way, what is most important tonight is to remember to have fun!

Blake Octavian Blair

April 3

Sunday

4℞ ≈
☽ v/c 7:16 pm

Color of the day: Orange
Incense of the day: Juniper

Releasing Unhealthy Beliefs about Sex

Today, the moon is a slender waning crescent, almost a Crone's sickle; and, as this is the month of Beltane, it's a good time to cast off old, archaic beliefs about sex and sexuality. Take some time to meditate on your sexual questions, and then research the answers, using reliable resources such as books and articles on healthy sexuality, rather than relying solely on the Internet, if at all possible.

Take a purple candle—the physical (red) manifestation of emotions (blue)—and carve it with statements of beliefs that no longer apply to you. As you light the candle, say:

As this candle burns down, as the moon wanes away, so let these old, outmoded beliefs wane and die a timely death. I am free from judgment and fear. So mote it be.

Thuri Calafia

April 4
Monday

4th ≈

$\mathcal{D} \rightarrow \mathcal{H}$ 1:45 am

Color of the day: Lavender
Incense of the day: Clary sage

Sacred Cybele

In ancient Rome, Cybele, the goddess of fertility, was celebrated with wild, orgiastic rites. Take inspiration from the Romans, and tonight celebrate sacred sexuality and creative fertility. Take precautions to protect yourself from pregnancy if that is not desired. Fertility isn't just about children, but about birthing and nurturing our "creative babies," too. Tonight, let the borders between love, sex, and creativity blur.

Whether alone or with a partner, honor and celebrate. While slowly undressing (your lover or yourself), admire each body part, gently stroking, whispering:

Beauty honors creativity.

Naked, stand before each other (or the mirror), uttering:

Thou art Goddess (or God).

Take time slowly touching and being touched, arousing your lover (or yourself). Move toward the bed, floor, or couch, then pause and invoke:

Cybele, bless us (me) and this sacred act. Our (my) pleasure celebrates fertile creativity. Let our (my) creative babies be born of this divine pleasure.

Dallas Jennifer Cobb

NOTES:

April 5
Tuesday

4th ♓
☽ v/c 6:33 am

Color of the day: White
Incense of the day: Ylang-ylang

A Money Spell

For this spell, you will need a green candle, a silver coin, and some moss—sphagnum moss from a garden center will do. Place the candle near the foot of the bath. Light the candle, and then fill the bath. Place the silver coin in your bath, and climb in. Submerge yourself in the water, and as you do, imagine yourself being covered with money luck. Emerge from the water, and say:

Silver coin that covers me,

Bless my life abundantly.

Do this three times. Don't use this bath for bathing—you don't want to wash the money spell away! If you can air-dry, great; if not, gently pat (don't rub) yourself dry, perhaps with a green towel. Put the coin on the sphagnum moss, and place this with the candle on your altar or other personal space. It's best if you can let the candle burn down on its own, but if you can't, then pinch or snuff it out—don't blow it! If you can wait until the candle has burned out before draining the bath, so much the better.

Charlie Rainbow Wolf

April 6
Wednesday

4th ♓
☽ → ♈ 2:46 am

Color of the day: Yellow
Incense of the day: Lilac

Unicorn Altar

It's Tartan Day, a day to celebrate Scottish heritage. Here's a little heritage to celebrate: Scotland's national animal is the unicorn. Unicorns are associated with purity, protection, beauty, elegance, subtlety, magic, intuition, shapeshifting, and connection with the Otherworld.

Today, build a unicorn altar, with the intention to align with one or more of these qualities. Keep it simple or get elaborate. You might paint, draw, print out, or find a unicorn image, and then add symbols as desired. For example, you could choose a feather for subtlety and/or intuition, and a white quartz or lepidolite for protection and/or purity. Light a white candle and diffuse a light floral scent (via oil or incense) such as lavender or lilac. Envision a wise and beautiful unicorn as a wordless invocation, and inwardly align yourself with his or her vast power and wisdom.

Tess Whitehurst

April 7
Thursday

4th ♈

New Moon 7:24 am

☽ v/c 10:56 am

Color of the day: Turquoise
Incense of the day: Clove

Black Mirrors

During the time of the new moon, many things remain hidden from our view. This is a great time to utilize scrying to see what normally cannot be seen. You will want to be in an area that is free from distractions. Your altar area would be ideal. Place a black mirror in the center of your altar, with candles and incense as far to the sides as possible to prevent their images from being reflected in the mirror. Now close your eyes and center your being. When you're ready, open your eyes and gaze into the mirror. Chant:

What is hidden can now be seen.
Reveal to me what I may glean.

Write down any images made clear to you during this time, as their importance may not be immediately clear.

Charlynn Walls

April 8
Friday

1st ♈

☽ → ♉ 2:10 am

Color of the day: Rose
Incense of the day: Alder

Apple Creativity Spell

For this spell, you'll need a fresh apple, a cutting board, and a knife. Hold the apple in your palms and close your eyes. Think of a project you want to do that requires creativity. See yourself inspired and working on the project with creativity flowing freely. See the momentum of your creativity growing, as each new step you take fuels the step to come. See the project being completed joyfully and to great success. Feel the power of your vision flow through your palms and into the apple. Open your eyes.

Cut the apple in half across the middle so that you can see the seeds in their star pattern. Eat the apple slowly, thoroughly chewing and swallowing each bite before beginning the next. As you eat the apple, each bite strengthens your drive and creativity. As you finish eating the apple, say:

As this apple fuels my body,
creativity fuels my mind.

Repeat the spell whenever you need a creative boost.

Emily Carlin

April 9

Saturday

1st ♉

☽ v/c 5:49 am

Color of the day: Blue
Incense of the day: Patchouli

Plant a Tree Spell

Now is a good time to plant a tree, and garden centers offer a big selection at this time of year. But why not put some magical effort into it? That will create a bond between you and the tree, and make it yours.

After you select a planting site, think about the kind of tree you want. Do you want a large shade tree, a fruit tree, or a small ornamental? After you decide, say words of power that you'll find the perfect tree for you. Once you get the tree home, water it well while still in the container or burlap; this shows the tree you care. After planting, press a penny into the soil as a sign of thanks. Then sprinkle a bit of your hair around the trunk as you say:

*With this coin and hair, we have a
special bond that we'll always share.*

James Kambos

April 10

Sunday

1st ♉

☽ → ♊ 1:59 am

Color of the day: Gold
Incense of the day: Hyacinth

For the Bees

Since there's a worldwide bee shortage, it seems like a good idea to work magic for their benefit, both to protect them and to bring healing. A simple way to lend them energy, both magically and physically, is to charm a plant so that the bees will have a place to gather pollen and will also absorb the magic. Good plants to use include sage, thyme, rosemary, or lavender.

To charm the plant, hold it and visualize emerald-green energy for nature and healing streaming from your hands into the plant. To direct the energy toward the benefit of the bees, seal your intent with this spell:

Plant of power, gift from earth,

Nourish their bodies; invigor, renew;

Heal to all, dis-ease reverse,

Strengthen the bees that come to you.

Place the plant in either a garden or an outdoor flowerpot to attract the bees.

Michael Furie

April 11
Monday

1st ♐ ♉

☽ v/c 2:57 pm

Color of the day: Ivory
Incense of the day: Lily

Revamp Your Altar

Take a good look at your altar, its decorations and setup. Is it still working for you? As we change and grow, so should our altars.

Add several drops of lavender and lemon oils to some water, and use this to clean your altar and everything on it. You are not only cleaning physical dust and dirt, but cleansing and recharging energy as well. Remove anything from your altar that no longer suits your needs or just feels out of place. Add any new items you want to include, cleansing them as well. Experiment with different setups. Rearrange items until the fit feels right. When you have everything in place, sprinkle a few drops of lemon and lavender oils directly on the altar. Bless it, saying:

This is my altar, where I do my spells, my rituals, my life's work. Bless my altar and bless me as well. This is my desire, so mote it be.

Kerri Connor

 April 12
Tuesday

1st ♐ ♉

☽ → ♋ 4:07 am

Color of the day: Gray
Incense of the day: Cinnamon

The Sky Is Not the Limit!

Today in 1961, Russian Yuri Gagarin was the first human to be launched into space. He successfully orbited the earth, awing people worldwide and opening minds to the expansive possibilities of the future.

Today, let us allow the anniversary of this event to inspire us to see the possibilities that exist in our own lives. Acquire a piece of citrine stone. Citrine is widely believed to have an energy of abundance and manifestation. Take a sheet of paper and write down three goals you'd like to accomplish, along with three action steps for each goal that you can take. These can be short- or long-term goals. Fold the piece of paper, and place it under the citrine on your altar. Place your right hand upon the stone, and visualize radiant energy flowing into the stone and your list. Periodically review your list and action steps as needed until you reach your goals.

Blake Octavian Blair

April 13
Wednesday

1st ♋

☽ v/c 11:59 pm

2nd Quarter 11:59 pm

Color of the day: Brown
Incense of the day: Bay laurel

Safe Travel Charm Bag

Are you starting to plan some fun trips for the upcoming season? How about making a charm bag for safe travel to tuck in your glove box? Use a small yellow pouch, organza bag, or piece of fabric about three inches square, with a ribbon to tie it shut. Draw a simple compass rose onto the pouch, bag, or fabric, and fill it with any or all of the following: fern, mint, comfrey, moonstone, clear quartz, a small image of Kwan Yin, or a crow. You may also include a found cat whisker (they fall out naturally from time to time), but never cut or pull off a cat's whisker, or the magic will have the opposite effect. Fill your charm bag and enchant it with the following intention:

Feel the magic build and grow,

To travel safely on the roads.

Protect this car and those inside,

Bless our travels as we ride.

Mickie Mueller

April 14
Thursday

2nd ♋

☽ → ♌ 9:53 am

Color of the day: White
Incense of the day: Mulberry

Spring Cleaning Spell

Spring cleaning accomplishes more than clearing cobwebs, dust, and grime: it's the perfect time to clear your home's stale energy and create a space to invite in new energies of possibility, prosperity, health, or whatever you need.

For this spell, you will need some coarse salt, rosemary, lavender buds, and a spray mist bottle with some water and a cleansing essential oil added (like lavender, any citrus, or any herbs like rosemary or basil). Mix the salt, rosemary, and lavender buds together in a bowl. Sprinkle the mixture in all the corners of your rooms, strewing a bit in a path along the walls, working clockwise from your starting point. Sweep or vacuum up this mixture, visualizing the dispersal of all negative energy. Then spritz the corners of the rooms with the essential oil spray, to "settle" the space and invite in positive energy. You can use rosewater to invite love, cinnamon for money, lavender for healing, basil for protection, etc.

Peg Aloi

April 15

Friday

2nd ♌

Color of the day: Purple
Incense of the day: Rose

Blessed by the Four Corners

The four corners (quadrants) and their corresponding elements are a strong foundation of Neopagan spirituality. They have been interpreted and reinterpreted through various cultures and traditions, though their archetypal essence remains the same.

If you desire a bit of extra elemental protection, consider blessing each room of your house with elemental tools. Aside from the traditional elemental tools (wands, pentacles, swords, and cups), consider other potential representations of the four elements. These could be feathers or sticks of incense for air (east), rocks or soil for earth (north), charred wood or lava rocks for fire (south), vials of water or seashells for water (west), or anything of your choosing—get creative!

Place your chosen tool(s) in their corresponding directions in every room of your house. Communicate with the cardinal directions as you do so; make this as fancy a procedure as you'd like. Visualize an etheric cord connecting each tool; this grid will help keep you energetically secure.

Raven Digitalis

April 16

Saturday

2nd ♌

☽ v/c 1:48 pm
☽ → ♍ 7:23 pm

Color of the day: Black
Incense of the day: Pine

April Showers Spell

The element of water encourages love, intuition, and clairvoyance. As we are in the month made famous for chilly spring rains, let's put a little of nature's natural magick to work, shall we? If it is raining, run out there and stand in it. If not, then pour some water into a clear glass bowl and dip your fingers in the water. Now scatter the droplets all around you. Say the following charm:

Whether it falls from the sky or drips from my hands,

April showers now do sprinkle across the lands.

Water encourages love and intuition to flow,

Now wash over me and my magick will bloom and grow.

By the element of water this spell is cast,

Happiness now flows to me and will surely last!

If you are outdoors, you may now go inside. If indoors, step outside and pour the water onto the earth.

Ellen Dugan

NOTES:

April 17
Sunday

2nd ♍

Color of the day: Yellow
Incense of the day: Frankincense

Summoning the Daffy-Down-Dilly Fairy to Make Your Garden Grow

Flowers are a fairy-fashionista's best friend, and there is none more showy or anticipated than the Daffy-Down-Dilly—the daffodil—the spirit of spring. Summon her to shake off any lingering vestiges of winter and bring life and blessings to your garden.

Find a patch of daffodils. At the base, place the items the Daffy-Down-Dilly will need to make and embellish her finery: tiny, shiny beads, glittering threads, or small, fluffy white feathers. Then call to her:

Daffy-Down-Dilly,

Come to my town!

Put on your green petticoat,

Put on your golden gown.

Show me your finery; show me your face,

Bring your friends and bless this space!

Leave similar offerings in your own garden or flower and herb pots, and watch the green world around you spring to life.

Natalie Zaman

April 18

Monday

2nd ♏

☽ v/c 8:29 am

Color of the day: Lavender
Incense of the day: Narcissus

Welcome the Sun Spell

Today is a sacred feast day to Apollo, Roman god of the sun. What better way to welcome spring than to honor the sun god? Solar energy is all about vitality, health, optimism, and energy, and we certainly need all of these after a long winter. Apollo was also associated with light (clarity of vision) and truth.

Make an altar to Apollo with any of the following objects: an Apollo figurine, a sun figure, gold coins or jewelry, jars of honey, yellow flowers, golden candles (beeswax is perfect), golden fabric, and golden fruit such as apples, lemons, or oranges. Arrange these objects in a pleasing way, to honor Apollo and invite his wisdom into your life. Gold is associated with prosperity, and the fruit and honey are related to health, longevity, and an abundant existence. The sun is at its zenith at noon each day; this is the perfect time to attune to the energies of Apollo.

Peg Aloi

April 19

Tuesday

2nd ♏

☽ → ♎ 7:24 am

☉ → ♉ 11:29 am

Color of the day: Red
Incense of the day: Bayberry

Blessing the Children

Today is my daughter's birthday, and while I bless and celebrate her, it's the perfect day to celebrate all children. Whether you are a parent, grandparent, guardian, neighbor, or friend of a child, and even if you don't have your own children, let's remember that it takes a village to raise a child, and that children everywhere need our blessings. Celebrate and bless the world's children with safety, security, nurturance, affirmation, and the ability to value themselves. Children need strong bodies, minds, hearts, and spirits, and powerful magic. Chant:

Like the earth, enduring and strong,

Let children's bodies be healthy, live long.

Like the fire's warming light,

Let children's minds be swift and bright.

Like the waters, healing and pure,

Let children's emotions and self-esteem be clear and sure.

*Like the air and wind that uplifts
and inspires,*

*Let children's spirits be vibrant
with desire.*

Blessed be the children.
                    Dallas Jennifer Cobb

NOTES:

April 20
Wednesday

2nd ♎

Color of the day: White
Incense of the day: Honeysuckle

Spell to Protect a Puppy

Even in Portland, Oregon, frequently voted the most dog-friendly city in the U.S., one will occasionally find aggressive dogs and irresponsible owners in the leash-free dog parks—such as the woman I recently encountered who, when asked if her dog was friendly, said, "I don't know, I just got him."

To protect your beloved pet, make an infusion of roses, lavender, mugwort, dragon's blood, and sweet alyssum. Soak a plain black cotton cord in the mix until the infusion cools and the cord is completely infused. Let it dry, then triple-braid it while chanting:

Lady Artemis, I ask of thee,

Protect this one who's dear to me.

Repel attackers, render them kind

*In emotions, actions, and all states
of mind,*

That s/he may play and safely run free,

And by our will, so mote it be!

Tie the cord around your dog's neck, leaving space for two fingers, as you would a collar. (As an alternative to the braid, you can simply soak the dog's collar in the herbal infusion.)
                    Thuri Calafia

April 21
Thursday

2nd ♎

☽ v/c 2:13 am

☽ → ♏ 8:17 pm

Color of the day: Purple
Incense of the day: Balsam

A Weight Control Spell

With summer near, many people become more concerned with their weight. Here is a spell that can help you with your goal.

You'll need a photo of yourself at your current weight and a pair of scissors. Every morning for three days, look at the photo and say:

The new me is already here.
It's inside me.

Then with the scissors, trim a little off your image every day. After the third day, place your photo on your altar.

Here are some tips. Set a realistic goal for yourself. Eat and exercise sensibly. When you're tempted to go off your diet, remember your spoken charm. And think of that new you hidden inside yourself. Every now and then, look at your photo.

James Kambos

 April 22
Friday

2nd ♏

🌕 Full Moon 1:24 am

Color of the day: Coral
Incense of the day: Yarrow

Earth Day

healing Earth Spell

For this spell, you'll need an empty jar, powdered milk, blue food coloring, and some dirt. As the moon rises, think of the healing thoughts you'd like to send to the earth and all her children. Fill the jar halfway with the powdered milk, and add a drop of the blue food coloring. Put the lid on the jar and shake it up, so the milk and the food coloring blend. This adds the healing energies. Open the jar and add a handful of dirt. Shake the jar again, saying:

The color blue from me to thee,

I honor and bless you, Mother Earth.

Empty the jar in a place outside that is special to you—under a favorite tree perhaps—and focus on pouring all that healing energy back into the earth, giving thanks. Keep a thankful heart as you finish your evening activities. The spell has been cast.

Charlie Rainbow Wolf

April 23
Saturday

3rd ♏

☽ v/c 5:46 pm

Color of the day: Indigo
Incense of the day: Magnolia

Passover begins

Wind Chime Storm Protection

April showers do bring May flowers, but they often rain down during some pretty intense storms. Here's a spell to calm the worst of the damaging winds and lightning when a storm reaches your house this spring. Anoint a wind chime with olive oil or lavender oil to instill peace and protection. Attach a small twig of ash somewhere on the wind chime. Charge the chime with its purpose:

Dangerous winds, I hear your knell,

Break up storms with ringing bells.

Blowing winds may be divine,

But powers of protection shall now be mine.

Your wind chime won't send back a storm or divert it, possibly causing more damage to others, but will knock the danger out of the storm, sending out ripples of protection as the bells ring. Use this spell with common sense, and be sure to follow safety warnings about incoming storms even with your chime in place.

Mickie Mueller

 ## April 24
Sunday

3rd ♏

☽ → ♐ 8:46 am

Color of the day: Amber
Incense of the day: Eucalyptus

Greet the Sun!

There are times when we need to recharge our spiritual batteries. One way to do so is to greet the sun.

Wake up with the dawn. Find a room that will provide light from the sunrise, or, if you are able to, go outside. Stand with your feet about shoulder width apart. Hold out your arms with your palms up toward the sun. Raise your face to the sun and close your eyes. Feel the warmth of the sun on your face and hands. Let the energy from the sun flow into you through your palms. Feel the warmth spread throughout your body. Now you are ready to take on the day and any challenges that may come with it!

Charlynn Walls

April 25
Monday

3rd ♐

Color of the day: Gray
Incense of the day: Neroli

Self-Cleansing Ritual

For this spell, you will need a crystal point and a bowl of sea salt. Cast a circle, using the crystal point as an athame. Invite the elements and deities of your choice.

Envision the negativity within you as black splotches. Pull all of the splotches together toward your center, then push the negativity out of you. Use the crystal point to direct the negativity to the bowl of salt to be grounded.

Thank the elements and deities. Open the circle. Dispose of the salt in running water, being careful not to touch it. Be sure to cleanse your crystal before using it again.

Emily Carlin

April 26
Tuesday

3rd ♐

☽ v/c 11:51 am

☽ → ♑ 7:54 pm

Color of the day: Scarlet
Incense of the day: Basil

Creating a Magickal Piggy Bank

Find a piggy bank, an opaque jar, or something else that can hold your extra money or savings—even if it's only accumulated pocket change! Dig in your pockets (or couch cushions) and find a quarter. Draw money signs and magickal symbols on either side of the coin with a permanent marker. Gaze intently at the coin and speak these words:

> In this vessel you're secure and stored,
> multiplying my abundance: more,
> more, more!

Place the coin in the piggy bank or jar; this should be the first piece of money you drop in. As you listen to the echo reverberate, imagine the sound ripples being sent through time and space to bring you the financial abundance you need to sustain your life. Be sure not to put your lucky coin in a vending machine; it should always remain in the vessel as the foundation of your spell.

Raven Digitalis

April 27
Wednesday

3rd ♑

Color of the day: Topaz
Incense of the day: Lavender

health Kick

Staying healthy isn't always easy, and weather really does play a part in how we feel, both physically and emotionally. Use this spell for healing or to keep yourself healthy.

Mix together the following oils: 6 drops of clove oil, 5 drops of lemon, 4 drops of cinnamon, 3 drops of eucalyptus, and 2 drops of rosemary. Drip onto a lit charcoal tablet in a fireproof container that you can carry around the house with you. Walk through each room of your home, allowing the smoke and scent to disperse. As you walk, say:

Cleanse this home and its inhabitants of any illness. Wash away sickness and disease, leaving only good health. Heal those who need it, and protect everyone who enters from ill health.

Repeat this over and over until you have walked through your entire home. Place the container on your altar and say:

Grant me this request.
It is my will, so mote it be.

Kerri Connor

April 28
Thursday

3rd ♑

Color of the day: Green
Incense of the day: Clove

Sunrise Violet Protection Spell

The violet is a faerie flower, and as we are in a waning moon phase, today's protection spell is perfectly timed. At sunrise, gather some violets from your yard, leaving a small offering to the nature spirits afterward. A little bird food will do the trick nicely. Then tuck the violets into a small glass of water or a tiny vase. Set these in a place of prominence in your home. Now hold your hands out over the flowers, and repeat the following flower fascination:

Violets, when gently at dawn they are plucked,

Do have the power to remove bad luck.

May the waning moon banish negativity from here,

While this faerie flower brings safety to those I hold dear.

I thank the faeries for their help with this charm,

This magick will unfold without trick or harm.

When the flowers fade, return them neatly to nature.

Ellen Dugan

April 29
Friday

3rd ♑

☽ v/c 3:07 am

☽ → ♒ 4:47 am

4th Quarter 11:29 pm

Color of the day: White
Incense of the day: Violet

Negativity Cleansing Mist

There are times when incense cannot be used but we need a way to cleanse the atmosphere of a negative vibe, such as when we are visited by an unwelcome guest. In this case, a spray can be made from cleansing herbs to break up the energy.

First, get a clean, empty spray bottle and a pot. Next combine one tablespoon each of basil, whole cloves, peppermint, and rosemary in the pot, and cover with two cups of water. Bring just to a boil, then remove from heat, allowing the herbs to steep, covered, for ten to fifteen minutes.

Once the liquid has cooled, strain it into a bowl and charge it as a potion to remove negativity. Pour the potion into the spray bottle and use as needed. To use, just spray in the air to diffuse any negative buildup in the immediate area.

Michael Furie

April 30
Saturday

4th ♒

☽ v/c 10:56 pm

Color of the day: Brown
Incense of the day: Patchouli

Passover ends

Body Image healing

Although Beltane is often said to be tomorrow, Beltane celebrations traditionally begin tonight—an evening also known as Walpurgis Night. Walpurga is an ancient Teutonic grain goddess who was honored on this day. Later, a Saint Walpurga appeared in Germany, and her feast day fell on May 1st.

With all of this in mind, this is an excellent day to work magic to heal food and body-image issues. Not only is Saint Walpurga said to help heal eating disorders, but faeries (whose realm merges with our own tonight, perhaps more strongly than on any other night) remind us to take pleasure in the sensual realm, which includes food, sex, and simply being in our own bodies. So tonight, light a candle to Walpurga. Set the intention to fully love and accept your body and appetites as they are. Anoint your belly, heart, and forehead with essential oil of jasmine, and dance the night away.

Tess Whitehurst

Anciently, in Western Europe, the year was divided in two: the dark half of the year, which begins at Samhain (October 31) and lasts until May Eve, and the light half, which begins at Beltane (May 1). The light half of the year is the more active time, when the energy of life is strong and waxing and we can look forward to the promise of summer. Since May begins one of the halves of the year, it is an initiator; similar to a cardinal zodiac sign, it shifts power to the new dynamic. The dynamic of May is one of fertility in plants and animals (including humans), birth, growth, and abundance. Of course, in the Southern Hemisphere, the opposite is true: May is the month that ushers in the dark half of the year, the time of rest, reflection, and renewal. Either way, the month of May is an important doorway into the second half of the year and a major energy shift. It is the polar opposite of its November counterpart in a beautiful dance similar to the concept of yin and yang, which is a wonderful focus for meditation.

Michael Furie

May 1
Sunday

4th ♒

☽ → ♓ 10:33 am

Color of the day: Gold
Incense of the day: Almond

Beltane

Beltane Ribbon Prayer Dance

Today is Beltane! While Maypole dances are traditional, we don't always have the resources or enough people to hold one. Here is a lovely alternative that is inspired by the spirit of tradition, but is part Maypole ribbon and part prayer flag.

You can construct a ribbon-dancing stick using a wooden dowel or tree branch, a length of ribbon several feet long, and an eyelet set from any craft store. Once you attach the eyelet set to the stick, and the ribbon to the eyelet, you are ready to inscribe onto the ribbon any magickal symbols or prayers you wish to make manifest. You can now hold the stick and ribbon in meditation, focusing on your goal. Then begin to dance, twirling the ribbon in celebration of the season and focusing on your intent. Your prayers are released into the wind as you spin, twirl, and dance!

Blake Octavian Blair

May 2
Monday

4th ♓

Color of the day: Gray
Incense of the day: Rosemary

A Catnip Love Spell

Catnip is a powerful love-attracting herb, and in May it should be growing well. With the Sun in Taurus, this is a good time to perform this spell.

You'll need two red candles, some catnip (fresh or dried), a few red rose petals, and a small red drawstring bag. Each night for a week, light the candles and sprinkle the catnip and rose petals in front of and around the candles. Push the candles a little closer together each evening as you say:

My heart is no longer alone.

I will find that special one.

On the last night, allow the candles to burn out, and gather the catnip and rose petals; place them in the drawstring bag. Hide the bag and tell no one about this spell.

James Kambos

May 3
Tuesday

4th ♓

☽ v/c 1:08 am

☽ → ♈ 1:04 pm

Color of the day: Maroon
Incense of the day: Geranium

Blessing Yourself
before an Undertaking

L ife itself is a Mercurial activity. We are constantly traveling, moving, communicating, checking and balancing, and otherwise shifting our energies as social creatures.

Before you engage in any big undertaking that concerns travel or communication, it's a good idea to invoke a bit of extra magickal mojo to help sustain you through the process. This simple working is a good way to prepare for a trip, a work-based commute, an important phone call, or a lecture or presentation you are to give.

After drying off from your morning shower, sprinkle a bit of cinnamon on your naked body. Next, use a natural ink to paint the alchemical symbol for Mercury (☿) on your body. I recommend painting the "horns" nipple to nipple, and have the "base" meet your belly button. When you enter a meditative state, visualize yourself glowing in a brilliant orange light and having a very successful undertaking. Vibrate "I-A-O" eight times vocally, and give thanks to Mercury.

Raven Digitalis

NOTES:

May 4
Wednesday

4th ♈

Color of the day: White
Incense of the day: Marjoram

Feel the Force

International Star Wars Day is more than a day to honor a story that took place "a long time ago in a galaxy far, far, away…" Since 2009, Jediism has been a recognized religion in England. The idea of the "Force" isn't just from a story. It is one of many names for the life energy that flows around and through us, making today an ideal time to use that energy to help manifest our desires.

Do this spell outside in a nature-rich area. Seat yourself comfortably, and close your eyes and relax. As you inhale, lift your arms out to your sides and then overhead, until your palms meet. Exhale and bring prayer hands down to heart center. Do this several times. Each time, feel the energy that is flowing around and through you. Feel the energy build as you draw it in and focus your intention on manifesting your desire. Continue breathing through this motion and focusing on your intention until you feel it is time to release the energy into the universe. Do this by raising your arms to the sky, and feel the energy shoot out of your fingertips into the world around you.

Kerri Connor

May 5
Thursday

4th ♈

☽ v/c 12:17 am

☽ → ♉ 1:10 pm

Color of the day: Crimson
Incense of the day: Carnation

Cinco de Mayo

Ancestor Altar

This day marks the victory of the Mexican army over the invading French, but for some reason the holiday is more widely celebrated in the United States than in Mexico. This would be a good day to reflect upon your cultural heritage. Do you know who your ancestors are? If you have any photos, letters, or other mementos, create an altar to display them and remember the people who are part of your identity. Think of the cultural struggles they endured. Did they come to the United States to escape poverty or persecution? Place some of the foods loved by your ancestors on your altar; maybe today you can prepare one of these dishes. Ancestor magic is very potent. It can help us feel connected to the deepest core of our being: the blood of those who came before us and who live in us. Keep this altar going, and add to it as you learn more about your ancestors.

Peg Aloi

May 6
Friday

4th ♉

New Moon 3:30 pm

☽ v/c 10:10 pm

Color of the day: White

Incense of the day: Yarrow

Hecate Shadow Spell

The dark of the moon is a special time for looking into the shadow side of things. Without the dark, we can't see the stars, so working with shadow helps us to see the sparks in our lives.

Use a black piece of paper and a silver pen, and light a black candle. List your fears that you want to manage in your life. Look over the list, and realize that the feelings brought up are temporary. Allow the feelings to pass through you. Once you have fully meditated on this, hold the black list of fears before you and state:

Mighty Hecate, light my path

As I examine my shadow's wrath.

I fiercely face what I must,

Embracing fears that turn to dust.

Light the paper and watch it burn, dropping it into a fireproof dish. Take the ashes and bury them far from your home or sprinkle them into moving water.

Mickie Mueller

May 7
Saturday

1st ♉

☽ → ♊ 12:35 pm

Color of the day: Black

Incense of the day: Sage

To Grow a Beautiful Garden

This is an amazing time of year for gardeners, and this spell can help give you and your garden an energy boost. You will need a teapot, some liquorice tea, and some peppermint tea. Make a big steaming pot of tea, and pour it into a large cup. Bring your tea into the garden, and think of all the wonderful things you're growing this year. Now take a sip for yourself, and swallow. Then take another sip for the garden—but don't swallow it. Spray it from your mouth onto the area that you're planting. In this way, you're not just putting the essence of the herbs on the soil, but you're also making an offering of yourself, blending your energy with that of the land. Your garden will reward you, for the more you look after it, the more it will nurture you with its bounty.

Charlie Rainbow Wolf

May 8

Sunday

1st ♊

Color of the day: Yellow
Incense of the day: Marigold

Mother's Day

Mother's Day Spell

Let's hear it for moms everywhere! There is little that is more powerful than a parent's love for their child. Being a mom is the toughest job you will ever love; however, it is totally worth it! Today, let's celebrate women and all their bewitching qualities with a Pagan blessing for the mothers in our lives. This spell verse could also be used to celebrate your own motherhood. On this solar-associated day, repeat this blessing under the light of the sun:

Motherhood is a sacred and joyous path,

My child/ren and I will enjoy a bond that lasts.

By the powers of earth, air, fire, and water,

May my love hold true with my sons and daughters.

May the Goddess always grant me wisdom, strength, humor, and love,

Illuminate my family's days like the sun up above.

Ellen Dugan

 May 9

Monday

1st ♊

☽ v/c 12:15 am

☽ → ♋ 1:24 pm

Color of the day: Ivory
Incense of the day: Narcissus

Harmonious Home Spell

Sometimes it's hard to get along with those closest to us, through no fault on anyone's part. For this spell, write down all the things that irritate you about a family member, roommate, or neighbor. Then, on another piece of paper, write down all the things you value about the person.

Burn the paper of irritations, reserving the ash in a small bowl. As the paper burns, say:

I release attachment to these emotions and hurts.

Take some lavender for peace and harmony, lemon for friendship, and sage for wisdom, and sprinkle them generously into the bowl of ashes. Imbue the mixture with love and understanding by reading aloud the list of all the things you love about the person while doing so.

Sprinkle the herbal mixture in any space that lies between the two of you. Make a promise to yourself to speak with that person as soon as

possible, to work things out. Stand your ground, but do so in kindness and compassion.

Thuri Calafia

NOTES:

May 10
Tuesday

1st ♋

Color of the day: White
Incense of the day: Cedar

La Virgen de Guadalupe

It's Mother's Day in Guatemala, El Salvador, and Mexico. This, coupled with the fact that the moon is in maternal, nurturing Cancer, makes it a good day to call on and align with one of the most beloved mother goddesses of our time: la Virgen de Guadalupe. Certainly, most Catholics would dispute her status as a goddess, but the worshipful devotion she inspires—as well as the fact that her first temple was built on the same site as the temple of the Aztec mother/earth goddess Tonantzin—would cause us to suspect otherwise.

Today, find a jar candle with la Virgen de Guadalupe's image on it, or simply make one yourself by attaching her image onto a jar candle. Light the candle and invoke the goddess, expressing your love and requesting support with maternal intentions such as comfort, nourishment, and support. Optionally, offer her a white rose.

Tess Whitehurst

May 11
Wednesday

1st ♋

☽ v/c 3:34 am

☽ → ♌ 5:32 pm

Color of the day: Topaz
Incense of the day: Bay laurel

Talking to the Trees

Trees have roots that travel deep into the earth and branches that reach high into the air. As such, they're often considered to be connected not only to the land but also to the heavens (or Overworld) and the Underworld. Before asking for magical assistance from a tree or harvesting parts of the tree, it is a good idea to establish a rapport with it.

To connect with a tree, simply touch it—the leaves, bark, branches, etc.—and send your energy into the tree gently so that it can evaluate your intentions and nature. Come to the tree with humility and honesty. I know this sounds silly, but the vibration of the tree will react to your energy. Speak to the tree, explaining your need. If you feel accepted, then gather only what you need and leave a gift in return. If you feel rejected, it's best to leave the tree alone.

Michael Furie

May 12
Thursday

1st ♌

Color of the day: Purple
Incense of the day: Jasmine

Dancing with the Moon

Monday is the day of the moon and one when its influences are keenly felt. It is easy to feel out of sync with the ebb and flow of the days and nights. In order to reconnect with the moon, go out after dark. The moon is just starting to grow and approaching its first-quarter aspect. It is still filled with potential energy. Reach your arms up toward the sky and embrace the possibilities. If you feel moved to dance in order to express this, then do so. Move in a slowly curving arc until you almost reach the point where you started. This honors the fact that even though we are in constant motion, we never really ever come back to the same point in our lives again. Take with you the knowledge that you have the same potential as the moon, and we are as ever changing as she is!

Charlynn Walls

May 13

Friday

1st ♌

☽ v/c 1:02 pm

2nd Quarter 1:02 pm

Color of the day: Coral
Incense of the day: Orchid

Sugar Cookie Friendship Spell

Friends are one of the things that make life worth living. You can help build new friendships and strengthen existing ones with this simple spell. You will need a recipe for sugar cookies and all the required ingredients, plus a place to bake them.

Prepare your oven and ingredients as your cookie recipe directs. As you do so, think about how you met the people with whom you wish to strengthen your relationship. As you combine your ingredients, think about the qualities you wish to cultivate in your friendships: understanding, empathy, trust, companionship, appreciation, etc. Let the energy of those qualities flow into the cookie dough. As you shape the dough into cookies, repeat the following mantra:

With understanding let friendship flow,
with sweetness let friendship grow.

Bake the cookies according to the recipe. Take them out when they're ready, let cool, and give them to your friends.

Emily Carlin

May 14

Saturday

2nd ♌

☽ → ♍ 1:52 am

Color of the day: Indigo
Incense of the day: Rue

Radiant Light

In Norway, today marks the beginning of ten weeks of perpetual light, with no darkness at night. The annual Festival of the Midnight Sun is held at sunrise, honoring the ancient Norse goddess of the sun, Sunna. Drawn by her horses "Very Fast" and "Early Riser," Sunna drives the sun chariot across the sky daily. Sunna is radiant light: bright, warm, and joyous. Her healing energy evokes peace and love.

Sit in the sun and invoke Sunna. With eyes closed, connect with her radiance. Breathe it in through your third-eye chakra, taking the dancing light up over your skull and down your spine. Exhale from your root chakra, the radiant light flooding into the earth. Each breath bathes the energy path with radiant light. Say:

Sunna, heal me with radiant light.
I'm a vessel of peace and love. I radiate
your lightness throughout the coming
days and nights.

Dallas Jennifer Cobb

May 15

Sunday

2nd ♍

Color of the day: Amber
Incense of the day: Heliotrope

A Spell for Increase

The sun is increasing in strength as we move toward summer. Tap into this solar energy and perform this spell to increase anything positive in your life. It could be a spell for career growth, material well-being, or even happiness.

You'll need three candles. Two should be votive candles in light and dark green. The third should be a pillar candle in orange or gold. This will be your sun candle. You'll also need to write your wish on a small piece of paper. Concentrate on your wish and light the green candles to represent growth. Next, light the sun candle. Watch the flame and say:

As the sun's power grows,
the power of my wish grows.

Ignite the paper in the candle's flame and let burn in a heatproof container. Sprinkle the ashes outside. Your wish has been released.

James Kambos

 May 16

Monday

2nd ♍

☽ v/c 5:20 am

☽ → ♎ 1:33 pm

Color of the day: Silver
Incense of the day: Lily

A Spell for Clarity in a Situation

It's easy to get discombobulated when life's drama unfolds. Emotional overreactions come easily when stress levels are turned on high. It's wise to practice grounding-and-centering exercises when challenging social situations occur. It's also a good idea to consciously direct energy to your own awareness in the midst of a difficult situation.

Get some of the herb eyebright (fresh or dried), and brew it into a tea. When it's at a comfortable temperature, drink the tea in silence and anoint your eyelids from time to time. You may even wish to wash your face and head with a cooled infusion of eyebright. Next, lie in a completely darkened room, and place the herb on your Ajna chakra (brow). Imagine its essence seeping into your third eye and into your conscious awareness. Repeat the word "clarity" until you feel the spell is complete. Finally, put some eyebright in two sachets and carry them in your pants pockets for one week.

Raven Digitalis

May 17
Tuesday

2nd ♎

Color of the day: Red
Incense of the day: Ginger

Crown of Victory

This is a spell to use when you want to build up your personal power. Light a gold candle anointed with cinnamon oil. As you light the candle, rub a little cinnamon oil on your palms, and hold your hands about a foot apart as you allow energy from your hands to pool between them into a ball. Envision the ball morphing into a crown before you. Visualize the crown with any details you like—the shape, jewels, symbols, etc., should be completely personal choices depending on your personality. Once you can see the crown completely in your mind, repeat the following:

Crown of Victory, my creation,

I summon you in this formation.

I have the power within my heart,

I embrace it through my Witch's art!

Grasp the crown and place it upon your head, and allow it to become one with your aura. You have given yourself permission to embrace your own power.

Mickie Mueller

 ## May 18
Wednesday

2nd ♎

☽ v/c 11:23 am

Color of the day: Yellow
Incense of the day: Lilac

Spell to Travel Safely

Despite modern innovations, travel seems more stressful now than ever before. With so many things to keep track of, added stress can make us forget important items or miss connections. Before traveling, make and wear this charm, and use it to focus your energy when things get overwhelming.

Take a square of blue silk or cotton fabric about 3 x 3 inches in size. Inside, place a small hematite stone, a silver dime or other silver coin (an antique coin made entirely of silver is best), an acorn, a small pine cone, a pebble, or some other natural object taken from the vicinity of your home, plus a small slip of paper on which you have written the word "HOME." Fold the fabric up around the object and paper, and tie the ends together firmly in a bundle with a piece of ribbon long enough to tie into a necklace. Wear this charm while traveling, and it will help you stay calm if any problems arise.

Peg Aloi

May 19
Thursday

2nd ♎

☽ → ♏ 2:29 am

Color of the day: White
Incense of the day: Nutmeg

Postcard Blessing

On this day in 1898, Congress passed legislation allowing private printers to print postcards for mailing in the U.S. It is said that this fueled the production and subsequent popularity of the picture postcard. In this day and age, with our ability to send an image instantaneous through e-mail, perhaps we should stop and pay homage to the nostalgic postcard. All of us still enjoy receiving tangible and fun mail from loved ones. Find a postcard that has an image of something you or someone dear to you holds sacred. I like to perform the following while sitting at my altar and burning a candle. Pen a short blessing to your loved one on the back of the card, thanking the person for their friendship or honoring a recent accomplishment of theirs. Draw one or more small sacred symbols on the back as well, to further magically charge your blessing. Now drop it in the mail!

Blake Octavian Blair

May 20
Friday

2nd ♏

☉ → ♊ 10:36 am

Color of the day: Pink
Incense of the day: Vanilla

Josephine Baker Day

In 1951, the NAACP declared May 20th "Josephine Baker Day." An American-born performer who was the toast of France and a highly respected muse to such giants as Ernest Hemingway, Pablo Picasso, Langston Hughes, F. Scott Fitzgerald, and Christian Dior, Josephine Baker's popularity as a dancer never took off the same way in the United States, due to prejudice and rigidly puritanical sensibilities. Still, her work as a civil rights activist was legendary: she accompanied Martin Luther King Jr. during the March on Washington, and she was the only woman to speak at the event.

Place a postcard or printed image of Josephine Baker on your altar today, and light a candle or some incense in her honor. Watch and post videos of her dancing, and vow to let your personal essence shine as brightly as she did, so that you can help inspire and change the world in the way that only you can.

Tess Whitehurst

May 21
Saturday

2nd ♏

☽ v/c 7:40 am

☽ → ♐ 2:48 pm

Full Moon 5:14 pm

Color of the day: Brown
Incense of the day: Patchouli

Milk Moon Divination

Do a bit of divination under tonight's Full Milk Moon.

Fill a bowl with milk and take it outside along with a blank piece of paper, a wooden skewer, and a piece of white ribbon. Catch the light of the moon in the bowl—if you can, try to catch the moon's reflection.

Take a moment to ground and center, then gaze into the moon-touched whiteness. Do any images, words, or anything else come into your mind? Don't think about them—write them down on the paper, using the milk for ink and the wooden skewer as a quill. Allow the milk to dry, then roll up the paper and tie it with the ribbon, knotting it three times.

Keep the scroll on your altar until the next full moon. Light a candle and hold the unrolled paper up to a flame to reveal the letters. Did any of your visions come to light?

Natalie Zaman

 May 22
Sunday

3rd ♐

Color of the day: Gold
Incense of the day: Juniper

Morning Self-Blessing

In the morning, just after you've gotten out of bed but before you've begun to get ready for the day, take a few moments to stretch out your body. Ground and center yourself and recite the following:

May the Gods be with me this day.

Help me to live, learn, and love as I should.

Help me to be all I can and should be,

And to do all that I can and should do.

Help me to refrain from being that which I should not be,

And from doing that which I should not do.

Help me to find my place in this world and to fill it;

To be happy and to thrive;

To be happy, healthy, wealthy, and wise.

So mote it be!

Emily Carlin

May 23
Monday

3rd ♐

☽ v/c 11:37 am

Color of the day: Lavender
Incense of the day: Clary sage

Quick Recharge

Summer is just around the corner, and the vacation season is at hand. The time needed to relax and recharge is an important part of life. Not everyone can afford an expensive vacation, but special events and day trips can provide a much-needed break, either free or at a low cost. Check sites like Groupon to find deals on interesting attractions. Treat your outing as a vacation. Plan for it and look at it as a break from your hectic life. Realize the importance of recharging your energy with a positive experience. Use this as a meditative encounter. Pay attention to how you feel before your "vacation" and compare to how you feel afterward. Make sure you spend your day enjoying yourself and not worrying about relaxing! Keep the goal in mind, but don't push it. Focus on the event, and the relaxation will come. Take it easy and have fun so at the end of the day you feel rejuvenated.

Kerri Connor

May 24
Tuesday

3rd ♐

☽ → ♑ 1:34 am

Color of the day: Black
Incense of the day: Cedar

Emerald Spell for the Coven

The emerald is the birthstone for the month of May. What makes this stone enchanting is that it encourages wisdom and communication between group members. During the waning moon tonight, perform this spell to banish negativity and keep your coven's energy on track.

Have every member of your coven acquire a low-grade emerald. (Low-grade emeralds are readily available and are perfect for this type of spellwork.) Now have everyone hold their emerald in their own hands and empower it with their personal power. Focus on improving the communication between the members of the group, and keep all thoughts positive! Then everyone say together:

May the lines of communication never falter,

Lord and Lady, watch over your sons and daughters.

By the small emeralds in our hands, this spell is now cast.

Negativity is banished, and harmony will last.

Have everyone keep their emerald as a token of friendship.

Ellen Dugan

NOTES:

May 25
Wednesday

3rd ♑

☽ v/c 9:11 pm

Color of the day: Brown
Incense of the day: Marjoram

A Nerdy Spell for Geek Pride Day

Today is Geek Pride Day, timed to coincide with the anniversary of the release of *Star Wars*, Towel Day (for fans of *The Hitchhiker's Guide to the Galaxy*), and the Glorious 25th of May (for fans of Terry Pratchett's *Discworld*). Geeks are smart, quirky, and fearless and are sure to succeed at anything to which they put their minds. Make a charm to invoke your inner nerd for atom-smashing success. On a piece of paper—or better yet, parchment, à la Hogwarts—write an affirmation spell using the elements as depicted on the periodic table:

I AM

B (Boron)

Ra (Radium)

I (Iodine)

N (Nitrogen)

Y (Yttrium)

Roll up the paper, seal it, and place it on your altar, computer, bookshelf, or crafting table. Speak the spell aloud to refresh the wibbly-wobbly. (Whovians, you know what I mean!)

Natalie Zaman

May 26

Thursday

3rd ♑

☽ → ♒ 10:27 am

Color of the day: Green
Incense of the day: Apricot

Summer of Love Spell

For this spell, you will need a heatproof receptacle, a small charcoal briquette for burning incense, and some dried lavender flowers.

Get the charcoal burning, and place it on the heatproof surface. When it is good and hot, add the lavender flowers. As they burn, picture yourself having fun and enjoying romance this summer. See how happy you are. Feel the joy that these scenarios bring into your life. Envision the smoke taking these images into the future, so that they can become manifest.

Once the flowers are burned and the charcoal has gone out, scatter them to the winds. Now go forward and live as happily as if you were already in this romance. The spell is cast—like energy always attracts like energy.

Charlie Rainbow Wolf

May 27

Friday

3rd ♒

Color of the day: Purple
Incense of the day: Violet

Live Long and Prosper

In ancient Rome, today marked the beginning of the Secular Centennial Games, and nighttime healing ceremonies honoring the *saeculum*, which was the longest-known duration of a human life (which was either 100 or 110 years).

We have evolved since Roman times, and these days people live longer, but today let's celebrate the saeculum. As you meditate, see the faces of the elders in your family and say silently or out loud:

May your every cell be well and healthy.

Visualize the elders in your community:

May your every cell be well and happy.

Envision your closest family members:

May your every cell be well and prosper.

Run your hands over your own body, from toes up to the top of your head:

May every cell be well and wonderful.
May all of my allies be well, healthy, happy, prosperous, and wonderful.

And, as Spock would say, may we all "live long and prosper."

Dallas Jennifer Cobb

May 28
Saturday

3rd ≈≈

☽ v/c 4:19 pm

☽ → ⊬ 5:06 pm

Color of the day: Blue
Incense of the day: Magnolia

Spell to Make Friends with Garden Fey

O ur gardens can be magical places, full of beauty and woodland creatures. But it is also possible to attract spiritual beings to these places. One great way to attract the fey (fairies, devas, sprites, etc.) is to leave out their favorite foods. They enjoy milk and all dairy products, sweets, wine and beer, and freshly made bread. Place a very small amount of fairy food on a plate and leave in a welcoming spot in your garden. Folklore tells us that the fey do not actually take the food away, but enjoy its essence/life force and leave the physical remains behind. (You may find that other garden creatures will enjoy these remains, so you can protect them from marauding squirrels with netting if necessary.) Leave the food and drink out at night on a regular basis (once a month or more). The fey are especially active at full and new moons and the cross-quarter days.

Peg Aloi

 May 29
Sunday

3rd ⊬

4th Quarter 8:12 am

Color of the day: Orange
Incense of the day: Heliotrope

Charm Bag to Banish Nightmares

B ad dreams can ruin the whole day. A fast fix for recurring nightmares is to make a charm bag with ingredients to ensure pleasant dreams. To create this charm, take a small square of fabric, preferably dark blue, purple, or black. Add a pinch of dried rosemary, anise seeds, and mullein leaves to the center of the fabric, plus some small citrine and amethyst stones. Hold the bundle in both hands while visualizing indigo-blue light streaming into it from your third eye. Tie the bundle shut with black cord to capture the energy. Focus the intent with this spell:

*Blocked and dissolved, the
nightmares end,*

Broken sleep does hereby mend.

Restoring peace and calm and rest,

*Through each night, my (their) sleep
is blessed.*

Place the bag under the mattress so it can radiate its energy without migrating around the bed.

Michael Furie

May 30
Monday

4th ♓

☽ v/c 7:10 pm

☽ → ♈ 9:09 pm

Color of the day: White
Incense of the day: Neroli

Memorial Day (observed)

Poppies for the Fallen

Memorial Day is a time for remembering those who have fallen in combat. You do not need to have known someone personally to communicate your thanks. You can honor those who have crossed over by creating your own red poppy to decorate your altar. You will need a small amount of red and black felt, along with some floral wire or green pipe cleaner. Cut out the flower portion from the red felt, and cut out a circle of black felt. Stack the two together, then cut or poke two small holes near the center. Place the wire up through one of the holes and then down through the other. Twist the ends together to create the stem. You can create one to honor all those lost in battle, or more if you have a more personal loss. Place the poppies on your altar with reverence while saying:

I remember and honor your spirit.

Spend some time in quiet contemplation and communion.

Charlynn Walls

May 31
Tuesday

4th ♈

Color of the day: Gray
Incense of the day: Geranium

Devotional Writing Spell for a Patron God

Whether you've yet to discover your patron god, have a new patron calling you, or have known your patron god(s) for a while, this spell will help you to express your devotion to him.

Carve an appropriately colored (to you) pillar candle with symbols or runes that remind you of your patron (or a patron you wish to connect with). Anoint the candle and light it.

Open yourself to the god's energies. Feel the connection between the two of you as the energy grows. Ask him how he would most like you to express your love for him. He may ask for poetry, a painting, or even a dance on this or the astral plane, or something else entirely. Give your gift as an offering to him. Be open to his guidance, and then express that devotional energy as often as possible to build and enhance your connection to him. Be blessed.

Thuri Calafia

June

The month of June is named for Juno, the principal goddess of the Roman pantheon and wife of Jupiter. She is the patroness of marriage and the well-being of women. This is one reason June is the most popular month for weddings. June brings the magic of Midsummer—the summer solstice, the longest day of the year. Summer is ripe now with bird song and the pleasant buzz of evening insects. The gentleness of spring has given way to the powerful heat of summer—the full moon of June is called the Strong Sun Moon. Various cultures pay homage to sun gods this time of year. In some places summer is just getting started and the hottest months are yet to come, yet after the solstice we don't even notice the days beginning to get slightly shorter. This is the time for enjoying the splendor of summer: playful picnics and hikes through the woods, long nights beneath the stars, tending gardens and flower beds. Roadsides are a riot of color, and herbs such as St. John's wort, vervain, and yarrow can be used in herbal amulets. This is the time of year to honor the faeries—leave offerings for them of ale, milk, fruit, or bread before cutting flowers or herbs, and they may help your garden grow.

Ember Grant

June 1
Wednesday

4th ♈

☽ v/c 11:42 am

☽ → ♉ 10:46 pm

Color of the day: Topaz
Incense of the day: Lilac

Wedding Blessing

It's no wonder that as the days become longer and the weather stabilizes, June is a popular month for couples to wed. Considering that the month June is derived from the Roman goddess Juno, and she was associated with marriage and married life, it is easy to see the basis of this long-standing tradition.

This blessing to the new couple could be written into a card for them or said as a toast:

May Juno see the abundance of your love and bless your union. Let it stand true and fast, being built on a foundation of trust and friendship.

Charlynn Walls

 # June 2
Thursday

4th ♉

Color of the day: Green
Incense of the day: Balsam

Macho Begone Spell

This spell must be done with humor and kindness! On a piece of paper, with a watercolor pencil or other water-soluble marker, write the heading "A REAL man…" and underneath it, list all the ridiculous notions you've ever heard about men or what men should be. As you do so, chant the words to the song "Macho Man" by the Village People, if you know them and are so inclined.

When the paper is finished, place it on a waterproof and fireproof surface on your altar. Sprinkle the paper lightly with water and watch the colors run, smearing them with your finger until they're dissolved or illegible, saying:

Foolish notion, false belief, begone, old macho, from the sight of me!

When dry, tear the paper into pieces (air) and burn it. Then bury the ash in the earth, repeating the chant. When you're finished, pat the ground over the ashes and say:

A REAL man is a human being!

Know that Mother Earth will recycle the energy into something nourishing.

Thuri Calafia

June 3
Friday

4th ♉

☽ v/c 7:02 pm

☽ → ♊ 11:01 pm

Color of the day: Pink
Incense of the day: Thyme

Origami Heart Spell

Infused with magical intent, objects made from a series of carefully executed folds—origami—can become talismans for change, protection, love, or whatever you intend them to be. Perform an origami heart spell to inspire or strengthen love. On a square piece of red or pink paper, write this incantation three times:

Love, come to me.

Fold the paper into a heart shape, repeating the incantation as you work. There are many methods of folding hearts; use your favorite reference to find one that you can execute with ease (such as www.origami-instructions .com/easy-origami-heart.html). Carry the heart with you and be open to receiving love. When love finds you, burn the heart in a ritual fire of gratitude.

If you are already part of a couple, do this ritual together. Make two hearts. Write your names on the origami sheets before folding them, then exchange them with your partner for safekeeping.

Natalie Zaman

June 4
Saturday

4th ♊

New Moon 11:00 pm

Color of the day: Indigo
Incense of the day: Patchouli

New Moon Dew Spell

Dew has been used for centuries as an aid to help increase the powers of prophecy. For this spell, you'll need a small clean jar with a lid, some bottled spring water, and an amethyst stone. Leave the jar outside overnight without the lid on. Early the next morning, while dew is still on the jar, bring the jar in and fill it with spring water. At this point, you may cap the jar and use the mixture later, or use it immediately.

When you're ready to use your dew mixture, anoint your third-eye chakra with it and wipe a small amount on your amethyst. Sit quietly while holding the amethyst, and think of a question you need answered. Close your eyes and see if a mental picture develops. Or wipe the amethyst with the mixture and place it under your pillow to induce a prophetic dream. Repeat during a new or waxing moon.

James Kambos

June 5
Sunday

1st ♊

☽ v/c 12:47 pm

☽ → ♋ 11:41 pm

Color of the day: Amber

Incense of the day: Marigold

A Spell for Vitality

For this spell, you will need some thyme (fresh or dried), a small square of red cotton cloth, and a length of red string or yarn. When the sun is at its highest, go outside and tie the thyme into the red cloth. Hold the amulet first to your head, then to your mouth, and then to your heart. As you do, say:

From the thoughts of my mind,

To the words of my mouth,

To the desires of my heart,

May I be strong in thought, word, and deed.

Put the amulet under your pillow at night, and let it rest in the sunlight during the day (on a windowsill or other place where it catches the light of the sun to recharge it) as long as you feel the need for extra energy.

Charlie Rainbow Wolf

 June 6
Monday

1st ♋

Color of the day: White

Incense of the day: Hyssop

Sleep Protection Spell

Recite the following just before going to bed while holding a sprig of lavender:

By the power of sun and moon,

I conjure.

Let the power of water come to me.

Encircle me.

Around me cast an impenetrable dream catcher.

Let nothing intending me harm come near.

Protect me.

Hide me from those of ill intent.

Let nothing disturb my rest.

Let me sleep in peace.

Let me wake when needed.

When I wake, the circle shall fade,

Until it is cast again.

Never let this spell reverse

Or upon me place a curse.

By nature's will and harm to none,

Let this my spell not be undone.

Place the lavender under your pillow and enjoy your rest.

Emily Carlin

June 7
Tuesday

1st ♋

☽ v/c 8:18 pm

Color of the day: Maroon
Incense of the day: Basil

Blessing a handfasting Cord

Since June is such a traditional time for weddings, it may be helpful to have a special spell to charge the cord used to bind a couple together for Pagan handfastings. In my tradition, it is customary to use a red cord, though some choose other colors such as white. Once the proper cord or ribbon is chosen, it can be blessed by holding it in the smoke of a good love incense, such as equal parts dried rose petals, myrrh, yarrow flowers, and cinnamon.

To focus the intent, say these or similar words:

Charged with power to forge the link; magic cord our love to bind, promises pledged, vows to keep, two souls joined and fates entwined.

The handfasting cord can then be stored in a natural cloth pouch for safekeeping until the day of the ceremony.

Michael Furie

June 8
Wednesday

1st ♋

☽ → ♌ 2:47 am

Color of the day: Brown
Incense of the day: Lavender

honoring the Rain Spirits

Whether we love or dislike rainy days, we know that they are vitally necessary. Belgium even has a saint of rain, Saint Medard, who is traditionally honored on this day. Although many of us probably don't work with Saint Medard, most cultures have a patron spirit of rain or weather who can and should be honored. Today, perform a simple offering and acknowledgment of these spirits in return for their overseeing of these life-renewing showers. Whether it is raining or not, open and set an umbrella on your lawn. Place under it, on a cloth or blanket, offerings as you see fit, such as things the rain helped birth to life: flowers, fresh fruits or vegetables, etc. Ring a bell or shake a rattle to summon the rain spirits and express your gratitude to them, and perhaps, weather permitting, perform for them a spirit-inspired dance or drumming.

Blake Octavian Blair

♪June 9
Thursday

1st ♌

Color of the day: White
Incense of the day: Mulberry

Dragon Boat Festival

Today is the Dragon Boat Festival, a Chinese celebration during which revelers race dragon boats and participate in rituals designed to protect their health. Common wisdom says that the festival honors the life of a historical figure (although the exact figure can vary by region), but there is evidence that its true origin was to honor the Dragon King of the region, or the Dragon Kings of the seas. Dragon Kings—ancient Chinese nature deities—symbolize powerful masculine energy, while also ruling the oceans and waters of the world. So, like the summer solstice, they embody the potency and balance of both poles: yang and yin, fire and water, the sun and moon. Today, throw a sunstone into a natural body of water as an offering to the Dragon King, a petition for health and inner equilibrium, and an expression of your appreciation for the waters of the world.

Tess Whitehurst

 ♪June 10
Friday

1st ♌

☽ v/c 3:14 am

☽ → ♍ 9:46 am

Color of the day: Purple
Incense of the day: Mint

Balance and Ground

Sometimes life gets out of whack. Everything you do seems to get messed up and you just feel off. Use this meditation to bring balance and grounded energy back into your life to straighten things out. If you can do this outside, great. Otherwise, you will need a bin of dirt, such as potting soil, if you need to do it indoors. If outside, find an area where you can dig up some dirt. Whether inside or out, add water to the dirt and make yourself a good mud. Stick your feet in it and work the mud with your toes. Imagine all the negative energy in your body being sucked out of you through the bottom of your feet and the tips of your toes. If you have some hematite, hold it in your hands. Imagine yourself being grounded and balanced with fresh, clean energy.

Kerri Connor

June 11
Saturday

1st ♏

Color of the day: Gray
Incense of the day: Sandalwood

Five-Minute Miracle

With sun and warm weather, gardens grow abundantly. Strawberries ripen, asparagus starts to fern, and rhubarb grows fibrous and ornamental. Pause for a moment today and give thanks for your garden's abundance. Whether your garden is a backyard plot, containers on a deck, or a pot on your windowsill, take a moment to appreciate the blessing of food, flowers, herbs, or vegetables that is yours. Soak up the joy. Now go! Perform a five-minute miracle.

Fueled by joy, move through your garden, gently nipping and pruning, pulling weeds, removing seed pods, and plucking off dried leaves. Fill a container with water and pour, soaking the plants with your gratitude, joy, and blessing.

Say:

You feed me joy, food, and flowers,

I feed you gratitude.

You bless me with nurturance, comfort, and nutrition,

I bless you with love.

You feed my spirit, heart, eyes, and belly,

I feed your sacred being.
Dallas Jennifer Cobb

NOTES:

June 12
Sunday

1st ♍

2nd Quarter 4:10 am

☽ v/c 10:47 am

☽ → ♎ 8:33 pm

Color of the day: Orange
Incense of the day: Almond

Red Rose Day Spell

Happy Red Rose Day! In the language of flowers, red roses symbolize love and romance. The rose is also the birth flower for the month of June. Here is a spell that encourages love and romance to come into your life.

Gather three fresh red roses, either from your garden or the florist. Arrange the roses in a vase filled with water, and set them someplace prominent. Take a moment to enjoy their color and scent. Breathe in the fragrance. Let it fill you up. Then repeat this charm:

By red roses three, I weave a charm,

For love and romance that brings no harm.

Allow this to come to me in the proper way,

As we all need love in our life, every day.

Keep the flowers in the vase until they begin to fade. Then return them neatly to nature or add them to your recyclable yard waste or compost pile.

Ellen Dugan

NOTES:

♪ **June 13**
Monday

2nd ♎

Color of the day: Gray
Incense of the day: Rosemary

Craft a Quill for Magical Writing

Feathery quill pens are the embodiment of air, the element that rules thoughts and ideas—the essence of spellwork. Think of how much more potent the words of a spell can be when they're written with implements made especially for that purpose. Find or purchase a feather to create a quill for magical writing. You'll also need a pen knife and a few craft supplies.

Use your favorite reference to trim the feather and shape the nib. (I use www.wikihow.com/Make-a-Quill-Pen-out-of-a-Feather.) Once the quill is cut and finished, paint or dye and decorate it. Use colors associated with the work you want to do: for healing spells, use a blue quill; for love spells, pink or red; for prosperity, green. Bless your quill before you use it:

From this quill

Flow my words.

And from my words,

Magic to (insert purpose).

Keep your quill wrapped in a dark cloth when not in use.

Natalie Zaman

 ♪ **June 14**
Tuesday

2nd ♎

Color of the day: Scarlet
Incense of the day: Bayberry

Flag Day

Spell for Getting Fit

Summer is here, and we want to look our best. It can be frustrating trying to lose weight when results come slowly. In addition to your chosen diet or fitness routine, try this spellworking to help see results. In your workout gear (or whatever clothes you exercise in), stand before a mirror. Look at yourself from top to bottom, and then look in your eyes and say:

I am getting fitter and healthier every day.

Do the same thing after you return from a session of exercise or after you've eaten a healthy meal. Do this to celebrate a milestone (an old pair of jeans fits again, or you increase the time or intensity of your workout) and at least once a day, regardless of whether you have exercise planned. This will help to remind you that you're making a positive effort and continuing to make progress.

Peg Aloi

June 15
Wednesday

2nd ♎

☽ v/c 3:00 am

☽ → ♏ 9:18 am

Color of the day: White
Incense of the day: Honeysuckle

Reclaim Your Voice

As we go through life, we become bombarded with so much input that we gradually forget to listen to our own true inner voice. Who are you? What do you stand for? What's important to you? The power to express your inner voice creates balance within you and helps you find your true path.

Begin your journey to reclaiming your true voice today. Obtain a piece of jewelry, ideally a necklace of labradorite, blue sodalite, or lapis lazuli. Meditate while holding the stone, and charge it with the intention. When you feel the stone fill with power, hold it to your throat chakra and allow nonsense words to come out—speak them, sing them, and let your voice ring out without judgment. Wear your piece of jewelry every day as a reminder to listen to your true voice and express it with love and confidence.

Mickie Mueller

 June 16
Thursday

2nd ♏

Color of the day: Purple
Incense of the day: Myrrh

The Magick of Faeries

As we near the Midsummer sabbat (summer solstice), this is an ideal time to connect with the subtle realm of faeries. If you haven't studied faerie lore or stories for a while, now would be a great time to brush up.

When you feel the pull to infuse your energy with that of the unseen world, gather the herbs elder, clover, thyme, sandalwood, and rose (or any combination thereof), and go to a sacred place in nature where you won't be disturbed. If you wish, wear sacred jewelry, glitter, and other "faerie garb" you deem appropriate.

As you enter the sacred place, let your imagination take control. Imagine that you are fae. Dart your eyes and prance nimbly around the terrain. Look everywhere for fellow faeries. Speak in a language your conscious mind does not understand. Let your creative innocence guide you to a new level of experience.

Afterward, take notes of your experience, have a shower, and come back to yourself.

Raven Digitalis

June 17
Friday

2nd ♏

☽ v/c 9:52 am

☽ → ♐ 9:34 pm

Color of the day: Coral
Incense of the day: Vanilla

Love Charm Spell

Stitch together two pieces of sheer red or burgundy fabric into a heart-shaped charm (or purchase a ready-made one from a craft store), and decorate it with satin flowers. Be sure to leave one side open, or use a drawstring. In a clear bowl, place dried roses, lavender, hyacinth, lilacs, and/or other flowers or herbs to invoke love, lust, friendship, prosperity, and any other loving quality you like. On top of the dried flowers and herbs, add powdered dragon's blood or other resins, and essential oils, such as rose, patchouli, or lemon. Fluff the mixture, imbuing it with your intent to draw the qualities inherent in the herbs and oils. When the power peaks, stuff the charm. Place on your altar, under your pillow, or on your person to draw sweet love into your life. This charm also makes a great wedding gift!

Thuri Calafia

 ## June 18
Saturday

2nd ♐

Color of the day: Black
Incense of the day: Ivy

Batten Down the Hatches

Everyone should practice good magickal hygiene. Renewing our personal barriers is a good practice to get into as we become worn down from daily stress.

In order to bolster your personal defenses, create a sachet that can be placed under your pillow or in your desk at work. Choose a variety of herbs and resins to place in a muslin bag. Some good choices would be amber, basil, bergamot, cinnamon, dragon's blood, nutmeg, sandalwood, and sea salt. Once you've created your personal mixture, envision your personal boundaries or aura as whole and complete while saying:

Renew my spirit and my barriers
for balance and protection.

Charlynn Walls

June 19
Sunday

2nd ♐

Color of the day: Yellow
Incense of the day: Eucalyptus

Father's Day

Spell to Embody Nurturing

Even if you do not have a good relationship with your own father, the concept of fatherhood can become a positive force in your life. You can become a strong and nurturing force in the lives of your friends and loved ones.

On seven slips of paper, write down seven different qualities you associate with a good, nurturing father figure—for example, affection, humor, or generosity. Put the slips of paper in a jar, and each day for a week, pick one slip of paper from the jar and embody that quality for the entire day in your interactions with others. See if you can offer the kind of strong and nurturing energy you associate with an ideal father figure.

Peg Aloi

 June 20
Monday

2nd ♐

☽ v/c 7:02 am

☽ Full Moon 7:02 am

☽ → ♑ 7:55 am

☉ → ♋ 6:34 pm

Color of the day: Ivory
Incense of the day: Lily

Litha – Summer Solstice

Reflection with the Fey

The summer solstice is perfect for working with the fey. Sometimes playful, sometimes malicious, these ancient creatures reflect our own human nature, especially the parts we don't like to admit exist. This spell helps us see that side of ourselves so we can take steps to fix it.

Do this spell under tonight's full moon. Sit on the ground, with a dark bowl of moon water in front of you. Sprinkle in a few drops of lavender and honeysuckle oils. Say:

> *Spirits of nature, guide me in my search for my true self. Show me that which I don't want to see about myself so that I may choose a new path.*

Gaze into the bowl, and slightly unfocus your eyes. Look for images of past events in which your attitude was not at its best. These visions are showing you where in your life you need to make changes.

Kerri Connor

June 21
Tuesday

3rd ♑

Color of the day: Black
Incense of the day: Cinnamon

Key to Your Future

When things in life get difficult, that's when you know you're about to level up! A door is about to present itself to you, and now you need to open it and step through.

For this spell, use a key, either an actual key that you don't use anymore or a piece of key jewelry. Anoint a red candle with frankincense oil, and roll it in black cohosh and thyme. Light the candle and hold the key as you focus on the flame. Enchant the key using this charm:

> The key to the future I hold in my hand,
>
> The direction I travel is in my command.
>
> Opportunities coming, good changes in store,
>
> I'll keep my key close to unlock my true door.

Leave the key near the candle as it burns down. The key is now a talisman to help usher you safely through the changes before you, so carry it with you.

Mickie Mueller

 ## June 22
Wednesday

3rd ♑

☽ v/c 4:57 am

☽ → ♒ 4:08 pm

Color of the day: Topaz
Incense of the day: Bay laurel

Summer Garden Charm

Hello, summer! The garden is in full swing, and flowers are blooming with abandon. Here is your chance to work a little garden magick and bless your plants, trees, and flowers so they will grow well for you over the next few months. This spell will work with either a container garden or a traditional garden. Go stand in the garden or next to all of your containers. Then repeat this charm:

> I now bless these trees, plants, flowers, and herbs,
>
> Elements four, gather round and hear my words.
>
> I seal this magick with the sound of a rhyme,
>
> My garden is enchanted for the summertime.

Ellen Dugan

June 23
Thursday

3rd ≈≈

Color of the day: Turquoise
Incense of the day: Jasmine

Knee-Deep in June Spell

This is a relaxation spell inspired by the poem "Knee-Deep in June" by American poet James Whitcomb Riley. Don't feel guilty about taking time to enjoy the beautiful month of June. Remember, we paid our debt by shivering in January!

First, combine a small amount each of basil, bay leaf, and mint. You'll use this as an offering to Mother Earth. Then go to a favorite outdoor spot where you won't be disturbed. Sit on the ground until you feel rooted to the earth. Now stretch out on the grass. Savor this time, and truly experience the blessings of the God and Goddess. Watch the clouds and look at the sunlight filtering through the trees. Smell the grass and listen to the birds. Don't think of anything in particular; just be in the moment. Let all stress be absorbed by the earth. As an offering, scatter the herbs about, and then leave.

James Kambos

June 24
Friday

3rd ≈≈

☽ v/c 11:48 am

☽ → ♓ 10:30 pm

Color of the day: Rose
Incense of the day: Orchid

Spell to Keep Bugs Away

Nothing dampens the mood of an outdoor event faster than getting eaten by bugs. This spell will help to keep them from pestering you without the use of chemical deterrents.

You will need a piece of cedar or a drop of cedar oil, a two-ounce bottle of natural vanilla extract, and a small (four- to eight-ounce) spray bottle. Place the cedar and the vanilla in the spray bottle, and fill it with water. Shake well, then mist yourself all over with the blend, envisioning the bugs leaving you alone and saying:

I mean you no harm, creeping crawlies of the earth,

But leave me alone to celebrate my mirth.

Reapply the mist as necessary, repeating the words again.

Charlie Rainbow Wolf

June 25
Saturday

3rd ♓

Color of the day: Blue
Incense of the day: Rue

Fairy Spell to Bless a Garden

If you have a garden, whether it's a large outdoor plot or simply a select group of potted vegetables, flowers, or herbs, calling upon the fairy kingdom to bless your plants with strength, growth, and magic can provide a noticeable boost to their health. This practice is also a simple way to build a working relationship with the nature spirits.

To work this spell, obtain a small fairy sculpture or toy that can be placed in the garden. Set the statue in the garden (or in one of the planter pots), and visualize the plants and fairy figure glowing with green energy. When your visualization is strong, call out to the fairies with these words:

Fairy spirits, hear my plea,

Nurture these plants and make them strong;

Enchant my garden, blessed be,

A sacred grove of mirth and song.

Leave small offerings of milk in the garden for the fairies.

Michael Furie

June 26
Sunday

3rd ♓

☽ v/c 3:55 pm

Color of the day: Gold
Incense of the day: Frankincense

The Piper's Allure

Many of us are familiar with the story of the Pied Piper of Hamelin, the mysterious musical figure who lured rats from a small German town, was denied payment, and exacted revenge by using his alluring music to draw the town's children away with him. While we can't be sure of the exact day this alleged event occurred, the German town of Hamelin still commemorates this story by celebrating Ratcatcher's Day on this date.

Let us take this day as an opportunity to acknowledge the power of music to enchant, allure, and transport us to other places and realms. In your own ritual space, play a recording of music that particularly accomplishes these goals for you, while you carry out a spellworking you feel called to do, or perhaps engage in ecstatic movement and dance to the music. Allow yourself to be transported!

Blake Octavian Blair

 June 27
Monday

3rd ♓

☽ → ♈ 3:08 am

4th Quarter 2:19 pm

Color of the day: Silver
Incense of the day: Hyssop

Jupiter Stator

In ancient Rome, the Temple of Jupiter Stator was dedicated on this day. *Stator* means "stayer" and refers to the time Jupiter assisted Roman soldiers in successfully standing their ground during a battle. With the moon in Mars-ruled Aries, today is a good time to set the intention to successfully stand your ground, whether you're feeling challenged by another person, a condition or situation, or your own seeming limitations. Cleanse two hematite stones in sunlight and/or sage smoke, and then empower them with a confident inner vision of remaining stalwart and emerging victorious. While standing near a large tree, invoke the sky god's assistance by chanting:

Jupiter, help me stand my ground and be the victor in this round. With the fortitude of this mighty tree, strongly rooted I shall be.

Place one of the rocks at the base of the tree, and carry or wear the other one until your victory is secure.

Tess Whitehurst

June 28
Tuesday

4th ♈

Color of the day: Red
Incense of the day: Ylang-ylang

Releasing That Summertime Sadness

Sadness is not something that's restricted to the autumn or wintry seasons. Generally, feelings of sadness mean that something is dying in your life—as difficult as it is, this means that new possibilities can come to fruition.

If you experience summertime blues, it's worth considering herbal medicine, behavioral modification, or even therapy in some cases. In addition to these suggestions, you can create your own spell by searching for autumn leaves in the summer. It's likely that you can find the tattered remains of some of these old leaves in the deep, dark corners of natural environments.

When you find these hidden remnants of autumn, remember that they—like your emotions—are engaging in a process of regeneration. Take a handful of these leaves and plant them at the base of a new houseplant, saying:

Seasons shift and so do I. These hindering feelings in me now die.

Raven Digitalis

June 29
Wednesday

4th ♈

☽ v/c 3:46 am

☽ → ♉ 6:03 am

Color of the day: Yellow
Incense of the day: Lilac

Vesta's house Blessing

Month's end is a common time for moving house. Whether you've sold and are moving to a new home, or you're a student leaving your college residence to return home for the summer, it's good to give thanks and remove your vital energy from the space, leaving it free and clear for the next inhabitant.

Light a candle and say:

I call on Vesta to bless this place,

Withdraw my energy and cleanse the space.

I've lived and grown and been happy here,

But I leave it now, free, joyous, and clear.

Walk through each room, feeling the joy of your experiences there. Symbolically gather up energy from each room with your hands, returning it to your heart.

Say:

I gather my energy from where I've lived,

And take it now, to my new home to give.

For the greater good.

Blow out the candle and leave the cleared space.

Dallas Jennifer Cobb

NOTES:

June 30
Thursday

4ℏ ♉

☽ v/c 8:19 pm

Color of the day: Crimson
Incense of the day: Apricot

Removing Obstacles to Prosperity

For this spell, you'll need one gold candle, a blank index card, and a gold or green pen.

Meditate on the kind of prosperity you want to bring into your life: money, professional success, strong friendships, etc. Then take a moment to think about the obstacles that prevent you from obtaining that prosperity, such as lack of opportunity, lack of will, outside interference, apathy, or unseen obstacles.

On one side of the index card, draw the astrological symbol for Jupiter (♃) and list the kind of prosperity you want. On the other side, list all the barriers you face, then cross out each one.

Light the gold candle and burn the card while saying:

Jupiter, I seek prosperity. Remove the
obstacles in my path with severity.
As I do will, so mote it be.

Let the candle burn out.

Emily Carlin

July

Oh, July… Sweet month of sun and flowers, the "Wednesday hump" of summer. In July, life is easy. The power of the Sun God is at its peak, and all is growing and flourishing, bursting from the earth as a gift of Beltane's fertility and heading inevitably toward the Mabon harvests as the Wheel makes its inexorable turns. In July, the flowers smell sweetest and the trees are the greenest as burgeoning life fuels our creativity and gifts us with long rapturous days, wild for the taking.

July is a wonderful time to care for your local faery folk. Create a small shrine for them in your yard or garden. Leave out a saucer with a bit of honey and butter—they will appreciate it, and may bless you with wisdom and joy. Keep some rue in your pocket to avoid being led astray by the faeries in one of their wilder moments!

You might also craft a protective summer herbal amulet. Gather either three or nine of the following herbs before sunrise: chamomile, clover, comfrey, ivy, lavender, mugwort, nettle, plantain, rose, rue, St. John's wort, sweet woodruff, thyme, wort, vervain, and yarrow. Dry the herbs in a cool, dark place for a few days, then crumble and use to fill a small pouch. Carry, wear, or keep your summer amulet nearby for blessings and protection.

Susan Pesznecker

 July 1
Friday

4th ♉
☽ → ♊ 7:44 am

Color of the day: Coral
Incense of the day: Violet

heat Spell for Dissolving Barriers

This spell is best begun in the morning. You'll need a crystal aligned to your goal. Clear quartz is an all-purpose stone, or you could choose from the following: rose quartz for love, aventurine for prosperity, bloodstone for legal matters, carnelian for protection, fluorite for luck, obsidian for grounding, moonstone for spirituality, or amber for healing. Charge the stone with intent—what you want to achieve, not the obstacle in the way. Place the stone in a container filled with water to cover the stone, then put in the freezer until solid.

Once frozen, take the container outside, setting it in the sun. Call to the sun:

Blazing heat of summer's glory,
obstacles do plague me now; dissolve
them with your fiery fury and set me
free to claim my goal.

Leave the container outside until the water is melted, and retrieve the stone as a charm for gaining your objective.

Michael Furie

July 2
Saturday

4th ♊
☽ v/c 11:43 pm

Color of the day: Black
Incense of the day: Ivy

A Spell to Burn Away an Enemy

Sometimes there are going to be people in your life with whom you just can't get along, and they seem to have nothing better to do than to try to make your life as complicated as possible. Ignoring them is the best plan of action, but that may not always work, especially if there is gossip involved. Malintent can be vicious, but you don't have to put up with this.

A strong and powerful way of severing all ties is to burn this person out of your life. I don't mean set the person on fire! However, try this. Write the person's name on a piece of paper, and take it outside. Using a magnifying glass and the light from the sun, set fire to the paper (in a safe place) and burn the name away. Keep burning until the paper is gone, then scatter the ashes to the wind. The tie is severed.

Charlie Rainbow Wolf

July 3
Sunday

4th ♊

☽ → ♋ 9:20 am

Color of the day: Yellow
Incense of the day: Almond

Establish harmony

It's a great day for clearing clutter, organizing, and bringing more beauty into the home. But first, create the proper atmosphere. Play soothing and uplifting music, diffuse essential oil of sandalwood, vanilla, and/or jasmine, and enjoy a delicious cup of sweet iced coffee or tea (decaf or herbal is fine if you don't do caffeine). Set the intention to establish comfort and harmony within, for yourself and all residents. Now, in a leisurely way, begin to clear, clean, and straighten your home as you feel guided. Don't strive to get it all done; just take your time and let the process be its own reward. You can always come back to it later. Perhaps attend to areas that you haven't cleaned in a while, such as your fridge or the floor of your closet. When you feel finished for the day, envision the golden-white light of harmony completely filling and encompassing your home.

Tess Whitehurst

 # July 4
Monday

4th ♋

New Moon 7:01 am

Color of the day: Lavender
Incense of the day: Neroli

Independence Day

A New Moon Liberation

A new moon on Independence Day calls for a spell to liberate and cleanse your life. Arrange three candles on your altar: one red, one white, and one blue. Red represents the life force, white symbolizes a fresh start, and blue represents peace and calm. Light the red candle and say:

I have the power to change my life.

Light the white candle and say:

A new path is before me.

As you light the blue candle, say:

I'll find peace.

On paper, write down whatever it is you wish to free yourself of. Snuff out each candle. Then take the paper to a running body of water, and place it on the water. Watch as the paper is carried out of sight. Say these words of power:

The problem I had will cease.
I'm liberated, I'm free. I'm at peace.

Leave your problem behind you. Walk away.

James Kambos

 ## July 5
Tuesday

1st ♋

☽ v/c 2:29 am

☽ → ♌ 12:28 pm

Color of the day: Red
Incense of the day: Ginger

Spell to Recover a Lost Item

Draw a quick sketch of the item you're trying to locate. Carve a taper candle with a few words describing yourself. Ground and center, then place the candle in the center of your altar, and anoint it from top to bottom, to pull energy in. Light the candle, envisioning it as your own inner light. Place the sketch a foot or so away from the candle on your altar. Then, as you move the sketch a little closer to the candle, say:

> My _____ is coming to me now.

Repeat this spell each night for three nights, moving the sketch closer each time, with it touching the candle on the last night. Pay close attention to any dreams or chance conversations that might give you clues to the location of the item.

Thuri Calafia

July 6
Wednesday

1st ♌

Color of the day: Topaz
Incense of the day: Honeysuckle

Messages to the Gods

Iris was a Greek goddess associated with the rainbow, as she provides a link between the realms of the sea and the sky. She was also a messenger goddess because of her ability to bridge the realms. She is an excellent choice to work with if there is a message you need help conveying. She can also take messages beyond the mortal realm. When a rainbow is present, or through the use of a prism, you can petition her help. Write your request on a piece of parchment. Then either while looking at a rainbow in the distance or while holding your prism, recite the following lines:

> Iris, goddess of communication, hear my need.
>
> Make haste and carry it with all due speed.
>
> Let the one that is meant to hear
>
> Be receptive to my message with an open ear.

Charlynn Walls

July 7
Thursday

1st ♈ ♌

☽ v/c 8:07 am

☽ → ♍ 6:41 pm

Color of the day: White
Incense of the day: Balsam

Star Light, Star Bright

Today, in Japan and China, two star festivals are held: Tanabata (celebrating the reunion of two celestial lovers) and Chih Nu (the annual feast of the Milky Way). Let these be your inspiration, and plan to get outside tonight for some star watching. If you live in a dense urban area, choose a park with lots of trees and little ambient light. Be safe: take a friend or two or three, plus a blanket, a picnic, and a pillow. Stretch out on your back, relax, and let the wonder of the starry universe dazzle you. Know that even in the darkness there are stars, and in the depth of life's problems there is light. As you gaze at the wonder of the night sky, intone:

Like the night sky, my future lies before me, vast, twinkling, and limitless. By starlight, I am blessed. So mote it be.

Dallas Jennifer Cobb

July 8
Friday

1st ♏

Color of the day: Pink
Incense of the day: Rose

Freya's Confidence Spell

Friday is the day of the week aligned with the planetary energies of Venus. Tonight you can combine the energies of the waxing-moon phase and the loving energies of a Friday (which is Freya's day) in your spellwork. This is the perfect opportunity to work a spell that draws beauty and confidence into your life.

To begin, light a pink candle, focus on your best assets, and visualize yourself standing tall, confident, and beautifully powerful—just like Freya herself (she was the leader of the Valkyries, after all!). Now repeat this charm:

Rosy pink candle burning warm and bright,

Lend your magick to mine on Freya's night.

With the magick of Freya, I spin this charm,

It boosts my confidence and causes no harm.

Now I'll walk in beauty and strength each and every day,

May this spell manifest in the best possible way.

Allow the candle to burn out in a safe place.

Ellen Dugan

NOTES:

July 9
Saturday

1st ♏

☽ v/c 11:28 pm

Color of the day: Gray
Incense of the day: Pine

Strengthen Boundaries

Boundaries help keep us safe, whether physically, mentally, or emotionally. Sometimes we let our boundaries slip and need to quickly build them back up. This spell is designed to help strengthen or rebuild the emotional boundaries you already have in place.

Dress a black candle with black pepper oil. Sprinkle some black pepper oil onto a sage smudge, and light it with the black candle. Smudge yourself in front of the black candle with the sage. Imagine the sage and black pepper building a wall around you, the sage on the inside, protecting you and keeping you safe, and the black pepper on the outside, repelling anything or anybody you don't want to get in. Make sure to thoroughly smudge yourself, or have a trusted friend assist you.

Kerri Connor

July 10
Sunday

1st ♏

☽ → ♎ 4:32 am

Color of the day: Amber
Incense of the day: Hyacinth

Ten of Wands Process Meditation

The Ten of Wands in the tarot represents reaping the harvest of a long process. It shows a figure who has collected a large bundle (the results of the process) and now must carry that bundle. However, how the person now deals with those results, good or bad, is up to him or her.

As we walk through life, it's important to remember that we are in a constant cycle of processes— some only beginning, others in progress— and yet also simultaneously ending other processes. It's important to foster the results we want, as we will be left to deal with them in the end.

Look at a version of the Ten of Wands, and meditate and visualize yourself as the figure in the card. See yourself reaping the harvest of a process. Taking into account your actions thus far, visualize what that harvest will look like. Further, once harvested, how will you proceed? Journal your experience afterward.

Blake Octavian Blair

July 11
Monday

1st ♎

2nd Quarter 8:52 pm

Color of the day: Silver
Incense of the day: Clary sage

Pearl of Wisdom

Pearls are a miracle of nature brought about by chance. A grain of sand finds its way into an oyster's shell. Irritated by the intrusion, the animal coats the grain with nacre, forming the pearl. The lesson we can take away from this process is that a negative experience can be made into something beautiful.

To activate this magic in your life, close your eyes and visualize a grain of sand. See it as a challenge you are facing, one that is uncomfortable but that you must live with. Cover that grain of challenge with a veil of white radiance. See and feel the grain soften and lose its abrasive edges, its ability to cause pain or discomfort. With every layer, repeat:

I surround you in love,

I surround you with myself,

Until I glow from within.

See the grain become a pearl. Repeat this meditation whenever you're facing a challenge.

Natalie Zaman

July 12
Tuesday

2nd ♎

☽ v/c 11:01 am

☽ → ♏ 4:52 pm

Color of the day: White
Incense of the day: Basil

Spell for Courage and Protection

For this spell, you will need these ingredients:

- Rue
- Devil's shoestring
- Cinnamon
- Mandrake
- A small carnelian bead
- A cotton tea bag
- Fiery Wall of Protection Oil
- A red candle and holder
- A tealight candle

Assemble all the spell components on your altar. Call in any protective deities or entities you're friendly with. Explain your situation and why you need courage and protection. Focus on that goal, and channel that energy into your spell components.

Put the herbs and carnelian bead into the cotton bag. Tie the bag shut using a triple knot, then tie the string around the bag to create a little package.

Anoint the candles with the Fiery Wall of Protection Oil. Light the red candle from a tealight, and put it in its holder.

Let the candles burn all the way down. Thank any deities or spirits you called on earlier, and bid them farewell. Now carry the bag with you until the situation is resolved.

Emily Carlin

NOTES:

July 11–18:
Best time to trim my hair for faster growth (during this Waxing Moon!)

Next full moon is 7/19

July 13
Wednesday

2nd ♏

Color of the day: Brown
Incense of the day: Bay laurel

Summer Purification Brew

This mixture can be drunk, added to baths for spiritual cleansing, or used to sprinkle with an asperger around an area to break up any negativity that may be present. These ingredients are easy to obtain, so this recipe can be used often. You will need:

- 3 cups water
- 2 sprigs fresh rosemary
- ½ cup sugar (more or less to taste)
- Pinch of salt
- ½ cup lemon juice (more or less to taste)

Pour the water in a pot, adding the rosemary, and bring to a near boil. Cover and remove from heat, allowing it to cool for fifteen minutes. Once cooled, add the sugar, salt, and lemon juice, stirring to blend. Hold your hands over the brew, visualizing white light pouring into it, charging it with purification energy. If you're using this to cleanse an area, omit the sugar, but you can use the rosemary sprigs as aspergers.

Michael Furie

(?)

July 14
Thursday

2nd ♏

☽ v/c 6:22 pm

Color of the day: Purple
Incense of the day: Clove

Obon

Kyu Bon marks the three days during which Obon—a Buddhist festival to honor one's ancestors—is celebrated in certain parts of Japan. Today is this festival's central day.

Tonight, create an altar with lit candles and images of a deceased loved one (human or otherwise) whom you want to connect with. You may particularly want to choose someone with whom you desire more closure or peace. Place a treat or meal on your altar that your loved one would have enjoyed during his or her life. Play uplifting music and dance as a way of transmuting negativity or heartache into joy and release. This will bring benefits to both you and your loved one. Afterward, smudge with sweetgrass to send your loved one's spirit into the most light-filled realm of the Otherworld. Extinguish the candles safely, and compost the edible offering or place it in a yard waste bin.

Tess Whitehurst

July 15
Friday

2nd ♏

☽ → ♐ 5:14 am

Color of the day: Rose
Incense of the day: Yarrow

A Self-Baptism Dedication

Baptism is not an experience reserved only for those of the Christian persuasion. Water has been seen as a cleansing and purifying source since the beginning of humanity, on both physical and metaphysical levels.

If you feel connected to a natural body of water, such as a gentle river, hot spring, or lake, carefully enter the water at a time when you can focus on yourself and your needs. Immerse yourself to your waist, and enter a meditative state. Reflect on your life to this point, realizing that everything is in a process of change—of death and rebirth. Find yourself aware of your body and aware of the water as a great cleansing force. Draw spirals on the surface of the water with your fingertips, whispering, over and over:

Cleanse me, purify me, renew me.

When you're ready, quickly (and carefully) submerge yourself, and then emerge as a purified soul.

Raven Digitalis

July 16
Saturday

2nd ♐

Color of the day: Blue
Incense of the day: Magnolia

Water Cleansing Meditation

One of the powers of water is that it has the ability to dissolve and erode. In the heat of the summer, being in the water is very soothing. It's a perfect time to use the power of water to dissolve away energies that no longer serve us.

You can go to an ocean, a river, or even your bathtub. If you're in a natural body of water, no preparation is necessary. If you're in your bathtub using tap water, you may wish to add sea salt or Epsom salt. As you soak, visualize dark flecks within your energy system releasing and floating free of your aura and being completely dissolved in the water, rendering them neutral. Free yourself of all anxiety, stress, and toxic vibrations of any kind. Feel the water lift them away, then visualize the water around you glowing in light as it creates a magical shield.

Mickie Mueller

July 17
Sunday

2nd ♐

☽ v/c 4:57 am
☽ → ♑ 3:33 pm

Color of the day: Gold
Incense of the day: Marigold

Spell for Cultivating Beauty

Maybe your neighborhood, house, or apartment building is a bit drab. You can inspire others by helping to beautify your surroundings, and remind yourself and others that beauty is a necessary and life-affirming influence. Get some annual flower seeds (easy-to-grow ones like marigolds, cosmos, nasturtiums, calendulas, and zinnias are all good choices), and plant them in sunny, well-drained soil in pots or in empty spots in your neighborhood. Don't forget to water them if the weather is dry. Meditate on the positive force of beauty every time you interact with these growing plants. When the seedlings appear, make sure they are not overcrowded. You may be able to transplant them to additional pots once they are a couple inches tall. Ask your local greenhouse to donate plastic planting pots for your project. Give extra pots of flowers to neighbors. Spread this natural beauty around everywhere you can. This is a simple but potent work of magic.

Peg Aloi

J**uly 18**
Monday

2nd ♑

Color of the day: Ivory
Incense of the day: Narcissus

A Spell to Stop Gossip

To stop someone from gossiping about you, you'll need a piece of paper with the person's handwriting on it. If this is not possible, get something the person has handled. You'll also need a jar, preferably an amber-colored one, plus a black candle and a brown paper bag. Put the paper with the person's handwriting on it in the jar, and put the lid on tightly. Light the black candle, letting the wax drip around the seal. As it does, say:

I bind your lips tightly,

That you'll not talk about me.

Place the jar in the brown paper bag, then take it in the direction away from the person who is talking about you—the farther away, the better—and put it in a dark place. When the gossip has stopped, remove the paper from the jar, and burn it along with the brown paper bag in which the jar was stored.

Charlie Rainbow Wolf

 J**uly 19**
Tuesday

2nd ♑

☽ v/c 6:57 pm

🌕 Full Moon 6:57 pm

☽ → ♒ 11:10 pm

Color of the day: Black
Incense of the day: Ylang-ylang

O Mighty Isis

Remember the TV show from the early '70s? Wonder Woman calling upon Isis and transforming into her super-heroine self?

Tonight, under the full moon, celebrate the birth of Isis, mother goddess of fertility, magic, and enchantment. Choose a safe space. Think of the multitude of roles you play in your day-to-day life: mother, daughter, sister, lover; brother, nephew, uncle, friend. In ritual space, face the moon. Strip off your clothes, letting go of the responsibilities of your mundane duties with each garment. Standing naked before the moon, call upon Isis like Wonder Woman did:

O mighty Isis, I am reborn tonight,
magical and enchanted, fertile, fierce,
and strong. I let go of doing. I embrace
being. I am me. And I am free.

As you put your clothing back on, pick up your roles and responsibilities, knowing that at the core of you is your super-heroine self—fertile, magical, and enchanted.

Dallas Jennifer Cobb

NOTES:

July 20
Wednesday

3rd ≈≈

Color of the day: Yellow
Incense of the day: Lavender

Moon Day Spell

Did you know there is a day of the year devoted to the moon? Yes, indeed. And that's today! Last night was the full moon, so those intense magickal energies are still with us. This is the perfect time to reaffirm your connection to the Lady Moon.

You will need a white flower, as all white flowers are associated with the moon. Then tonight, as the moon rises, stop and honor the power and the magick of the moon with these words:

Today is the day devoted to the moon,

Goddess, hear my call and grant me a boon.

Bless my magick and my Witch's craft,

May our bond be one that truly lasts.

As a token, I offer you this white flower,

My thanks I send to you in this magickal hour.

Ellen Dugan

July 21
Thursday

3rd ≈≈

☽ v/c 9:56 pm

Color of the day: Crimson
Incense of the day: Carnation

Let the Sun Set on Your Troubles

Bring a Ten of Cups tarot card outside at sunset, along with a gold or yellow candle. Turn the card face down next to the candle, then light the candle while watching the sunset. Think about any troubles that are weighing on your family right now. As you feel these troubles building up within your heart, allow them to flow down your arms and into your hands. Once they've filled your hands, hold your hands open before the sunset and blow your troubles into the sun. Whisper:

Mighty fire, blazing sun,

Take my troubles with you,
as the day is done.

As you watch the sunset, your troubles are burned up in the sun. Flip over the card and view the happy, peaceful image. After you're done watching the sunset, let the candle burn out and place the card somewhere in your home. Your troubles will begin to work themselves out.

Mickie Mueller

July 22
Friday

3rd ≈≈

☽ → ♓ 4:35 am

☉ → ♌ 5:30 am

Color of the day: White
Incense of the day: Cypress

Finding Partnership

"No man is an island," or so the saying goes. We all must enter into various partnerships in our lives, be they with friends, business associates, family members, or lovers. This spell will help you find the partnership that is right for you.

On one side of a fresh sheet of paper, list all the qualities you're looking for in a partner. The pen color should reflect the type of partnership you seek: red for love, orange for business, green for family, and yellow for friendship. On the other side of the paper, write all the qualities you will bring to the partnership. Make sure these lists are balanced, so that the relationship the spell draws will be equally balanced.

Roll the paper into a tube, and tie it with a ribbon of the appropriate color. Place the tied paper on your altar for a moon cycle, then burn it.

Emily Carlin

July 23
Saturday

3rd ♓

Color of the day: Brown
Incense of the day: Ivy

Flower Healing

If you need an energetic tune-up or spiritual guidance of any sort, try visiting a guru of the garden: a blossom. Once you find one that feels right (growing or cut), sit or stand comfortably near it and consciously relax your body as you come fully into the moment. Gaze at the blossom lovingly, and just take in its unique beauty and presence. When it feels right, present your challenge to the flower in the form of a feeling (flowers communicate on the level of emotion), and request healing and guidance. Then just continue to relax and enjoy the beauty of the flower. In time, whether you consciously realize it or not, the flower's energetic pattern will merge with yours, and you will experience deep shifts on many levels: mental, emotional, spiritual, and physical. When this feels complete, say a heartfelt thank you to the blossom, and go on your way.

Tess Whitehurst

 ## July 24
Sunday

3rd ♓

☽ v/c 3:06 am

☽ → ♈ 8:33 am

Color of the day: Orange
Incense of the day: Frankincense

Spell to Discover the Nature of Sacrifice

Take a black candle and hold it while pondering all you have given up so far this year in order to achieve the goals you set out to accomplish. This might be personal time, money, or energy spent on reaching your goals. Try to imagine what your year would have been like had you not made the sacrifices you've made. Now ponder the same energies regarding your whole life, acknowledging that even the difficult times had their purpose, whether it was in helping you grow stronger or more knowledgeable in some way, or sending you in a needed direction.

Carve symbols on the candle representing your sacrifices. Breathe deeply as you do so, keeping yourself calm and centered. Light the candle, saying:

I'm open to understanding why these sacrifices had to be made.

Acknowledge your personal deities' best wishes for you and the evolution of your spirit. Be blessed.

Thuri Calafia

July 25
Monday

 July 26
Tuesday

3rd ♈

Color of the day: Lavender
Incense of the day: Rosemary

Tree Pose Meditation

When life gets out of whack and off-kilter, sometimes the best way to restore balance is with a little sympathetic magic. If your life is out of balance, shift it back into balance by using actual balance! Tree Pose is excellent for bringing the body into balance, and while you practice this physical act of balance, allow your mind to work at bringing yourself into mental balance as well. To do this pose, draw your foot up and place the sole against the inner thigh of your other leg. Be sure to switch feet and practice using each leg as a sturdy tree trunk holding you up, powerful and strong. When you switch legs, shift your focus from meditating on mental balance to meditating on emotional balance. Practice this pose often, so the strength in your legs improves and gives you a good, strong foundation to support yourself while you do the meditative part of this exercise. The longer you can hold the pose physically, the longer you can work on the mental and emotional aspects.

Kerri Connor

3rd ♈

☽ v/c 2:19 am
☽ → ♉ 11:37 am
4th Quarter 7:00 pm

Color of the day: Scarlet
Incense of the day: Geranium

Justice

Today is a good day to tune in to the strength of Mars if you have a matter of the law or one of fairness to take into account. Pull out your favorite depiction of the tarot card Justice, which brings a balance to all things. Set the card on your altar in the morning hours, and meditate on it. Look at the card's depiction and take in its details. What is it trying to convey to you? Refer back to the card throughout the day. At day's end, sit in front of the card again. Think back to the events that occurred throughout the day, and try to remember if any of the symbols from the card presented themselves to you. What was the context of those occurrences? Put together a list that you can refer back to later.

Charlynn Walls

July 27
Wednesday

4th ♉

Color of the day: White
Incense of the day: Marjoram

Find a Feather

The symbolism of nature directly connects to the conscious mind. If you need a bit of energetic renewal today, try seeking out a feather. Feathers represent the element of air, whose qualities include clearing, cleansing, and beginning anew.

Set some time aside to go on a nature walk. Find a feather that calls your name. Once you've gotten home, place the feather on your altar and imagine it glowing in soft yellows and whites. Contemplate the bird from which the feather came, and bring to mind its symbolism of freedom and flight.

Slowly brush the feather up your body, toe to head, then back down your body from head to toe. Burn some natural incense, and waft its smoke around your body. Say aloud:

Free as a bird, this message is heard:
I cleanse my life of pain and strife.

Conclude the ritual by burying the feather outside and giving thanks.

Raven Digitalis

 ## July 28
Thursday

4th ♉

☽ v/c 11:13 am

☽ → ♊ 2:17 pm

Color of the day: Green
Incense of the day: Myrrh

Spell for a Bountiful Harvest

The fields and orchards are just starting to burst forth with fruits and vegetables. Make sure your goals and projects are well tended, too. Each day, place some freshly picked or harvested produce (berries, flowers, greens, etc.) on your altar. You may place it on a dish and eat it later, or put in a vase for decoration. Try to cultivate your awareness of growing things as you watch them grow and bear fruit, and imagine your own work bearing fruit. Look at the produce on your altar and say:

As the season yields its bounty, I give
thanks and know that my own hopes
and dreams will bring a rich harvest.

This can be helpful if you're looking for a new job, a new relationship, or a new social activity to enjoy. Harvest and prosperity magic are closely related, but appreciating the harvest is also about showing gratitude for all you have.

Peg Aloi

July 29
Friday

4th ♊

Color of the day: Pink
Incense of the day: Vanilla

Universal Buzz

We encounter insects every day. Sometimes they're a welcome presence, and other times…well, it depends on the bug, doesn't it? There are no accidental encounters. Insects have symbolic traits that can be interpreted as messages from the universe. Should you encounter a…

- firefly, be yourself to attract what you desire into your life.

- ladybug, your wish will soon come true!

- bee, work as a team.

- ant, work hard!

- fly, think and act quickly.

- earthworm, know that even the smallest efforts are important.

- centipede, it's time to move forward!

- butterfly, get ready to transform.

- moth, listen to your dreams.

- mosquito, find what you need by paying attention to details.

- gnat, be persistent!

- cockroach, adapt to survive and thrive.

- spider (technically not an insect), work at your own pace and create something beautiful.

Thousands of creatures are waiting to communicate with you. Interpretations will vary depending on your tradition, culture, and experience.

Natalie Zaman

NOTES:

July 30
Saturday

4th ♊

☽ v/c 7:46 am

☽ → ♋ 5:09 pm

Color of the day: Indigo

Incense of the day: Sage

Reclaim Your Closet

Saturday is a good day energetically for tending to the home. Amid the bustle of a full life, we often let some housekeeping slide. Clutter accumulates, and a bit of disorganization sets in. For many of us, closets are especially prone to clutter—applying the adage "out of sight, out of mind." But modern feng shui consultants say the state of one's closet often mirrors the organization and order in the rest of one's home and life. So in a dual clutter- and chaos-clearing effort, take some time today to clean out and organize a closet in your home. Even if other tasks have to wait for another day, reclaiming control of this unseen space can energetically bring a new sense of peace into your home. When you are finished cleaning the closet, you can ring a bell in the closet or waft some smudge smoke in it to energetically zap any residual stagnant energy.

Blake Octavian Blair

July 31
Sunday

4th ♋

Color of the day: Amber

Incense of the day: Juniper

Pot of Gold Spell

The Sun is in Leo and the harvest is about to begin. Use these energies to draw prosperity to you. For this spell, you'll need a cauldron, a dollar bill, a money-attracting herb such as dill, three plastic gold toy coins, and a gold or orange cloth. Begin by placing the dollar into the cauldron, and sprinkle the herb over it. Drop the coins in one at a time. Each time you add a coin, say:

Herb and dollar green,

Coins of gold,

Bring me all the money

That my pockets will hold.

Then cover the cauldron with the gold or orange cloth. Give the spell time to work. When prosperity manifests itself in your life, sprinkle the herb outside. Save the gold coins for another spell, but hide the dollar and never spend it.

James Kambos

August

The eighth calendar month is full of the last hurrahs of summer (or winter, if you're in the Southern Hemisphere). Originally the sixth month of the Roman calendar, August was known as Sextilis until the Senate changed it to Augustus sometime around 8 BC. This was in honor of Augustus Caesar. August was full of holidays. The month started with a public festival honoring Spes, the goddess of hope, and ended with the Charisteria, a feast at which to give thanks. Most of the deities honored in August were fertility and harvest gods. The Anglo-Saxons referred to August as Weod Monath (Weed Month) or Arn-monath (Barn Month). In the Northern Hemisphere, August marks the start of the harvest season festivals, with the celebration of Lughnassad, or Lammas, on the 1st. August starts out in the constellation of Leo, a fixed fire sign, and moves into Virgo, a mutable earth sign, around the 20th. The birthstone of the month is peridot. Interesting fun fact: no other month starts on the same day of the week as August unless it's a leap year, in which case August and February start on the same day.

Laurel Reufner

August 1

Monday

4th ♋

☽ v/c 8:44 pm

☽ → ♌ 9:12 pm

Color of the day: Silver
Incense of the day: Lily

Lammas

Breaking Bread

Lammas marks the first festival of harvest. We celebrate the fertility of the sacred union of the Mother Goddess and Horned God with bread, because *Lammas* comes from the Saxon words *blaf mas*, or "loaf mass."

Tonight, celebrate fertility, harvest, and community bonds by breaking bread with allies—people who support and care for you. Honor relationships where the sacred, fertile union produces positive social, emotional, and spiritual fruits for all.

Plan a simple meal: bread and butter, soup, salad and homemade dressing, wine, ale, or grape juice. Welcome your allies by name. Light four candles on the table to invoke the elements. Hold up the loaf of bread and say:

I salute you, friends, allies, tribe.

I invite you to break bread and imbibe.

I'm rich with your friendship, love, and grace.

Let the fruits of our friendship bless this place.

Let us feast.

Eat, drink, and celebrate the harvest of belonging.

Dallas Jennifer Cobb

NOTES:

August 2

Tuesday

4th ♌

New Moon 4:45 pm

Color of the day: White
Incense of the day: Cinnamon

New Moon in Leo Prosperity Spell

Now that the harvest season has officially begun, it's time to reap the rewards of all our hard work throughout the year. A simple spell for prosperity can include herbs aligned with the sun (the ruler of Leo). Fill a gold-colored charm bag with one tablespoon each of chamomile, cinnamon, dried orange peel, and sunflower seeds. Visualize golden light streaming from your third-eye chakra into the bag to charge it, and say:

Prosperity and abundance, gather to me,

Through the power of sun and moon;

For good of all and blessed be,

Money increase with magical boon.

Seal the bag and carry it with you.

Michael Furie

August 3

Wednesday

1st ♌

Color of the day: Brown
Incense of the day: Lavender

Commemoration of the Myrrhbearers

The Lutheran Church recognizes August 3rd as the Commemoration of the Myrrhbearers, Joanna, Mary, and Salome: the women who famously visited Christ's tomb with fragrant myrrh, and found it empty. Myrrh was also one of the gifts that the magi famously brought to the manger. What do a manger and a tomb have in common? Bad smells. Indeed, myrrh was not only a treasured spiritual perfume, but also a means of overpowering an undesirable odor and changing an unfortunately pungent earthly atmosphere into a spiritual and transcendent one.

So today, if there is an aspect of your life that (metaphorically) stinks, describe it in writing on a piece of paper. In a cauldron or fire pit, safely light the paper on fire. As it burns, light three sticks of myrrh incense and smudge the flames with the fragrant smoke as you imagine the challenge transmuting into pure, sweet-smelling positivity and beauty.

Tess Whitehurst

August 4

Thursday

1st ♌

☽ v/c 12:13 am

☽ → ♍ 3:34 am

Color of the day: Crimson
Incense of the day: Nutmeg

A Spell of Memory and Mind

Both walnuts and nutmeg (if cut open) look like little "brains." This, in a symbolic sense, allows us to perform sympathetic magick with these tools in order to target any issue having to do with the brain, such as memory.

Get a walnut and some nutmeg (ground is okay), and mix them in a sachet bag with rosemary. Rosemary is renowned for its magickal property of mental fortitude. Once you've blended these together, tie the bag shut and deeply inhale the scent of the contents. Balance the bag on your head and put your hands in the Anjali Mudra (prayer position) at your heart. Repeat aloud:

My mind is ignited; I stand in awareness.

When you feel grounded, take the bag from your head and hold it between your palms. Imagine its energy directly connecting to your brain, helping you through any situation that requires concentration and focus. Smell the bag whenever you need this spiritual inspiration.

Raven Digitalis

 August 5

Friday

1st ♍

☽ v/c 11:20 pm

Color of the day: Purple
Incense of the day: Cypress

happy, healthy home

Mix together four drops each of lemon, lime, orange, grapefruit, peppermint, and lavender oils, and two drops of black pepper oil in a large spray bottle filled with moon water. (To make moon water, place a glass bowl or bottle of spring water outside under a full moon overnight.) This combination will help cleanse, purify, and protect your home, to keep it happy, healthy, peaceful, and filled with positive energy. Walk clockwise throughout your home spraying the mixture high into the air in front of you as you go. Shake the bottle often to keep the potion well mixed. As you spray, repeat the following:

Bring happiness, good health, and positive energies to my home.

Say this over and over as you spray continuously. Make sure to spray high and into the corners of each room. Spray inside of closets and cupboards, and be sure to reach all areas of your home, including the pantry, attic, crawlspace, or basement, if you have one.

Kerri Connor

August 6

Saturday

1st ♏

☽ → ♎ 12:57 pm

Color of the day: Blue
Incense of the day: Rue

Cinnamon-Star Money Grid

The sun is in Leo and the moon is waxing; it's a great time to work magic to increase prosperity. Tap into this energy with a money grid for your altar. You'll need twelve cinnamon sticks, twelve star anise, plus four coins and a dollar bill in any denomination.

Place the bill on your altar and write the word "GROW" on it. Form four triangles over the bill using the cinnamon sticks; the apex of each triangle should point in one of the four directions: north, south, east, and west. Cap each angle with a star anise, then place a coin in the center of each triangle. Speak this prosperity-drawing incantation:

By the power of three times three,

By coin, stick, and star,

Grow, multiply, and come to me

From near, from far.

Repeat the incantation every day, and keep the grid intact for as long as you need.

Natalie Zaman

August 7

Sunday

1st ♎

Color of the day: Orange
Incense of the day: Heliotrope

Purification

Purification rites are completed in order to purge the unclean or undesirable aspects of one's self. The purpose is to make yourself clean and pure. Today, cleanse your body by drinking large amounts of water. You can also consume spicy foods, which will help the body cleanse itself. During the day, connect to the power of the phoenix, which rises from its own ashes. Carry with you a picture or pendant of the phoenix to remind you that you can become more than you once were, if you just expel what is not needed.

Charlynn Walls

August 8

Monday

1st ♎

☽ v/c 1:41 pm

Color of the day: Gray
Incense of the day: Hyssop

Discovering Your Place in Your Local Community

Sometimes when we're new to a community or spiritual path, we're uncertain of where we stand within that community. Take a piece of cardstock and draw lines dividing it into several sections in a puzzle pattern. In each section, write a different community-service action you might be interested in doing or see a need for in your community (for example, doing divinatory readings, teaching a workshop, etc.). Leave a few of the sections blank, in case your gods want you to rest, heal, or serve them somewhere else—in those cases, it's best to build your skills and energy before moving on.

With the puzzle before you, close your eyes and hold your left hand, palm down, over the puzzle. Take your time and move your hand over the entire puzzle slowly. Whenever you feel a warmth or tingling, take a marker and quickly make a mark on that piece. Try not to get focused on the places you've marked, but just keep sweeping your hand until you've gone over the whole area.

Once you've gone over the whole puzzle, open your eyes and see which service activities your subconscious chose. Meditate on how you can get started on these actions, and choose one or two to start, adding more as your energy and your confidence in your community grow.

Thuri Calafia

NOTES:

August 9
Tuesday

1st ♎

☽ → ♏ 12:51 am

Color of the day: Maroon
Incense of the day: Ginger

A Personal Harvest Spell

This spell celebrates the personal harvests in your life and also allows you to thank the Goddess for your good fortune. On your altar, place the Empress card from the tarot. On each side of the card, place an orange candle. You should also have a few kernels of grain—corn, wheat, or barley are good choices. On a piece of paper, write the names of three people or things in your life for which you're grateful. Then light the candles. As the flames grow, sprinkle the grain over the paper and say:

*Goddess, I thank you for these things
I have. And I thank you for the bounty
still to come.*

Let the candles burn a while, then extinguish them. Save the grain and your list. Review your list at the end of the year, and add to it if you need to. Then burn the list and feed the grain to the birds.

James Kambos

August 10
Wednesday

1st ♏

2nd Quarter 2:21 pm

Color of the day: Yellow
Incense of the day: Bay laurel

Abracadabra Obstacle-Shrinking Talisman

Remember those sheets of shrinking plastic you put in the oven as a kid? Seemed like magic, right? Here's a cool talisman made from recycled plastic that you can make and enchant to remove obstacles. Watch for plastic packaging marked #6; you probably have something from the grocery store packaged in it. Find an image of a diminishing abracadabra, with the word repeated with one less letter until it disappears. Place a clean piece of #6 plastic over your image, and trace the design using a permanent marker, visualizing what you want to diminish in your life. Bake the plastic on a parchment-covered cookie sheet at 350 degrees F. for 2–3 minutes. It will curl up as it shrinks and then lie flat. As it shrinks, chant:

*Obstacles shrink from me, with
harm to none, so shall it be.*

Keep it as a talisman to ward away your chosen obstacle.

Mickie Mueller

August 11

Thursday

2nd ♏

☽ v/c 1:22 am

☽ → ♐ 1:24 pm

Color of the day: Turquoise

Incense of the day: Carnation

A Friendship Spell

This spell is designed to help you infuse an existing friendship with love and understanding, so that your relationship with the person may remain steadfast and full of joy. You'll need a pink candle, a pink ribbon, a white ribbon, a lavender ribbon, and a photograph of your friend.

Focus on the photograph and light the candle. Reflect on all that you and your friend have shared over the years. Reach out to this person with your heart, and keep focusing on the flame of the candle until you feel your heart full of your friend's presence. At that time, take the three ribbons and braid them together: the pink one for love, the white one for purity, and the lavender one for understanding. When you're finished, extinguish the candle, and put it, the ribbons, and your friend's photo in a place of safekeeping.

Charlie Rainbow Wolf

 August 12

Friday

2nd ♐

Color of the day: Rose

Incense of the day: Yarrow

All Is Well

During August's blazing heat, it's easy to feel like summer will last forever. We don't notice the days growing shorter, the nights getting cooler, and the winds blowing stronger. Change is subtle and may register first in our spirit as an irksome feeling of dis-ease. While the sun shines bright and warm, acknowledge this "cooling" feeling. Embrace change. Wrap wellness and warmth around you, and prepare for what is to come. Envision yourself wrapped in a bright blanket of sunlight. Draw this warm cloak close, and walk confidently into the future. Chant:

All is well, I'm safe and secure.

All is well, I'm healthy and nurtured.

All is well, I'm guided and protected.

All is well, I'm loved and accepted.

All is well, as seasons change,

I now adapt and rearrange.

All is well, in this world, I belong.

I am resilient and safe,
I am warm and I am strong.

Dallas Jennifer Cobb

August 13
Saturday

2nd ♐

☽ v/c 1:37 pm

Color of the day: Gray
Incense of the day: Magnolia

Shadow Invisibility Spell

For this spell, you'll need a small black tourmaline stone.

Whenever you wish to move about at night unnoticed, hold the tourmaline in your hand and recite the following:

On this night and in this hour,

I call upon the ancient powers of shadow and mist.

Wrap around me.

Hide me from prying eyes.

Let me fade.

Unnoticed.

Unnoted.

Unseen.

I'm not here now.

Chameleon-like,

I am unseen.

Until I will to be seen again.

Carry the tourmaline where it can touch your skin. When you're ready to release the spell, say:

My spell is done.

From it I wean.

Reveal me now.

I can be seen.

Use the same stone repeatedly for better results.

Emily Carlin

NOTES:

August 14

Sunday

2nd ♑

☽ → ♑ 12:11 am

Color of the day: Gold
Incense of the day: Eucalyptus

Crafting Magickal Rowanberry Necklaces

Rowanberries, which are prevalent on rowan trees at this time of year, can be used for numerous magickal and metaphysical purposes, in addition to having the potential to be used in homemade marmalade and a variety of medicinal remedies.

The rowan tree is also known as the Witch tree. One of the most relevant magickal uses of the berries is that of recapitulation. This refers to the process of energetically "pulling back" your energy that may be stuck. It's common for people's energy to get stuck in certain places and on certain people.

To aid in your own visualization work aimed at drawing back your essence, try threading a number of rowanberries with a needle and tying off the end to form a necklace. Wear this whenever you're feeling overwhelmed with life or whenever you are performing any deeply personal healing work or personal shamanic journeying.

Raven Digitalis

 August 15

Monday

2nd ♑

☽ v/c 10:45 pm

Color of the day: White
Incense of the day: Neroli

Letter to an Ancestor

Today is the main day of the Japanese Bon Festival and is referred to as Hachigatsu Bon. The Bon Festival is a celebration of one's ancestors, and traditional celebratory activities include dancing and the visiting and cleaning of ancestors' graves. Tradition also holds that ancestors may visit the homes and altars of loved ones.

Let today serve as a reminder and opportunity for you to communicate with your ancestors. Gather a pen, paper, a fireproof bowl or cauldron, and a white candle with an appropriate holder. Light the candle, then sit down and pen a letter to a departed loved one. When you've finished writing, fold the letter in thirds, then write your loved one's name on the exterior. Now light the letter in the candle's flame and drop it into the cauldron as it changes form into smoke and sends your message into the ethers. So mote it be.

Blake Octavian Blair

August 16
Tuesday

2nd ♑

☽ → ♒ 7:52 am

Color of the day: Gray
Incense of the day: Cedar

Spell for Clarity

Fill a clear glass bowl with water, and place it on your altar. Carve runes or other symbols for clarity (or even simply write the word "clarity") on each of a pair of white taper candles, and place them on either side of the bowl. Ground and center, and think about what it is that has you confused. Pour a small amount of clean black sand (such as the kind you can obtain at a craft store, or regular sand you've previously washed) into the water, and stir it with your finger, chanting seven times:

Muddy is the water, muddy is my way,
beloved Lord and Lady, bring me
clarity today!

The last time through, repeat from "beloved Lord and Lady" three times, to seal the spell. Light the tapers and say:

As the moon grows, as the light shines,
so the clouds part, clarity is mine!
So mote it be.

Thuri Calafia

August 17
Wednesday

2nd ♒

Color of the day: White
Incense of the day: Marjoram

Moon and Sun Charm

Tomorrow the moon is officially full; however, we can and should work with the moon as it rolls into its fullest phase, and tap into all of the burgeoning energy. Tonight, as the moon begins to rise just before sunset, work your magick while both the sun and moon are in the sky together. Use these lines to open your own spellcraft. Happy casting!

As the sun sets, so does the waxing
moon rise,

I'll work magick now while they're
both in the sky.

By the powers of both the moon and
the sun,

As I will it, and let my magick
harm none.

Now work your own magick, and blessed be.

Ellen Dugan

August 18
Thursday

2nd ♒

☽ v/c 5:27 am

Full Moon 5:27 am

☽ → ♓ 12:34 pm

Color of the day: Green
Incense of the day: Apricot

house Blessing

For this spell, you will need the following items:

- Saltwater
- Incense
- Milk and honey
- Bayberry oil

Begin in the living room. Cast a circle around yourself, then expand it to encompass the entire house (or apartment). Invite whichever energies you would like to be present.

Go through the entire house, and at each entry, sprinkle saltwater and cense with incense, saying:

> With the power of the four directions,
> I purify and charge this entry.

Then anoint the entry with milk and honey, saying:

> I offer milk and honey to ensure peace
> and prosperity in this place.

Then, with the oil, draw an invoking pentacle and say:

> With this oil, I seal this portal and
> protect all within.

When you get to the front door, do the same, but at the end add:

> Friends will always be welcome at my
> door, but by nature's will, let none
> intending harm pass this threshold.

Open the circle.

Emily Carlin

Notes:

August 19
Friday

3rd ♓

Color of the day: Pink
Incense of the day: Orchid

Spell to honor the Salem Witch Trials' Victims

This day in history marks the execution by hanging of five prisoners accused of witchcraft during the infamous Salem witch trials. This horrific injustice was the result of a convergence of superstition, community upheaval, prejudice, jealousy, and attention-seeking behavior. Light a candle on your altar for each of these five victims, speaking their names aloud, one by one:

George Jacobs Sr.
Martha Carrier.
George Burroughs.
John Willard.
John Proctor.
You are pardoned, and we honor your memory. May we never again experience such tragic loss of life through ignorance and fear.

Write their names on a piece of paper, and place it upon your altar. Meditate on the significance of this injustice as it applies to our current problems. How many others have been victims of "witch hunts" or superstition-driven persecution? Remember them on this day, too.

Peg Aloi

August 20
Saturday

3rd ♓

☽ v/c 8:21 am
☽ → ♈ 3:18 pm

Color of the day: Black
Incense of the day: Ivy

Abundant harvest

If you're a vegetable gardener, by now you've been harvesting all kinds of good, fresh food from your garden, but the season isn't over yet! The early harvesters are winding down, but those plants that take longer to mature are now starting to produce. Some still have plenty of time to grow and still need plenty of care, such as tomatoes, squash, potatoes, and carrots.

Place a geode at each corner of your garden to encourage fertility and abundance. Add several drops of black pepper oil to moon water in a squirt bottle, and spray around the border of your garden or around the sides of planters. (To make moon water, place a glass bowl or bottle of spring water outside under a full moon overnight.) If you have a large garden, you can add actual finely ground black pepper to a hose feeder and spray this around the border instead. The black pepper is for protection and will also help keep some pests away from your veggies.

Kerri Connor

August 21

Sunday

3rd ♈

Color of the day: Yellow
Incense of the day: Juniper

Save Your Seeds Spell

If you have a garden, it's great to save seeds from your plants so you can plant the following year without investing in seeds. Another benefit is that by using seeds of your own harvest, you keep the cycle of abundance going in your life without breaking it, and the magic just builds year after year. Gather flowers, vegetables, or herbs that have gone to seed, and collect the seeds in small envelopes or zip-lock bags. Be sure to mark them so you know what they are. Place them on your altar with some of your current harvest, and light a beeswax candle. Bless your seeds:

> By seed, sprout, stem, blossom, and fruit,
>
> I bless these seeds to soon take root.
>
> From my own bounty, I gather potential,
>
> For next year's planting shall
> be monumental!

Store your seeds in a cool, dry place, and don't forget about them next spring!

Mickie Mueller

 August 22

Monday

3rd ♈

☽ v/c 7:48 am

☉ → ♍ 12:38 pm

☽ → ♉ 5:19 pm

Color of the day: Ivory
Incense of the day: Clary sage

What Lies Beneath: Invoking the Element of Water

What lies beneath the water, that powerful elemental linked to our emotions? Befriend this spirit with a waterside ritual. Stand at the edge of a body of water (or use a bowl of water). Sing or chant:

> What lies beneath the surface
>
> Is what lies beneath my skin.
>
> There is water and me.
>
> It is my kin.

Build a small tower of stones or shells in the water, or make a chain of flowers or leaves and toss it in as an offering to the life that lies beneath the rippling surface. Dip your hands in the water and sprinkle it over your head three times. If you perform the ritual with a bowl of water, tip any plants, stones, and remaining liquid onto the earth after you've blessed yourself.

Natalie Zaman

August 23

Tuesday

3rd ♉

Color of the day: Red
Incense of the day: Bayberry

Practical Bibliomancy

If you're drawn to magickal and mystical paths, it's likely that you own a number of books. Let your intuition guide you to three books of your choice. These books can pertain to any subject matter and can be new or old, fiction or nonfiction, big or small.

Enter a sacred space and, in your own words, summon the spirits of vision and divination. Ask that your ancestors, guides, and guardians be present. Bring to mind three separate questions, and write them on a piece of paper. Close your eyes and grab one of the books while you verbally ask your first question. Randomly flip to a page and point to the section that you're guided toward. Open your eyes and write the sentence, paragraph, or image you encounter. This is your "answer."

Repeat this process for the other two questions. Once completed, reflect on the abstract responses to see how they somehow symbolically correspond to the questions you've proposed. The answers may surprise you!

Raven Digitalis

August 24

Wednesday

3rd ♉

☽ v/c 3:38 pm

☽ → ♊ 7:40 pm

4th Quarter 11:41 pm

Color of the day: Topaz
Incense of the day: Lilac

Candle Spell for Improved Learning

Since this is the time of year when many people, from children to college students, return to school, a spell to improve learning can be helpful to start things off properly. This being Wednesday, Mercury's day, makes it a perfect time for mental improvement. You will need the following items:

- Yellow candle
- Carving tool (pin, nail, or knife)
- Rosemary oil

To begin, carve the name of the person who is the subject of the spell into the candle, and anoint it with the oil while visualizing a yellow aura surrounding the person, who is studying with ease and success. As you light the candle, say:

Mental focus and memory,

Boosted, strengthened, and empowered;

Through your learning, you will blessed be

And grow in knowledge, hour by hour.

With harm to none, by free will,

For the good of all, my wish fulfill.

Allow the candle to burn for as long as is safe and desired.

Michael Furie

Notes:

August 25

Thursday

4ħ ♊

Color of the day: White

Incense of the day: Clove

Spell for Runic Work

This day marks a Nordic festival celebrating the discovery of the runes. If you use runes, this is the perfect day to divine meaning from them, or to begin such a discipline in your magical practice. You may purchase runes or make them yourself. To get them ready for divination, you can bless them with the elements: air, fire, water, and earth. Combine air and fire by lighting some loose incense on a charcoal block, and pass the bag of runes through the incense smoke. Combine water and earth by making saltwater, and sprinkle this lightly on the runes to cleanse them. Place the runes in a dish on your altar, perhaps positioning them near other items charged for your magical work such as tarot cards, crystals, or jewelry. Let the runes remain upon your altar all night, then use them the next morning to do some divination work.

Peg Aloi

 August 26

Friday

4ħ ♊

☽ v/c 8:30 pm

☽ → ♋ 11:06 pm

Color of the day: Coral

Incense of the day: Rose

Cornucopia of Abundance

Celebrate the harvest season by acknowledging the abundance of the season. Place seasonal vegetables or fruits around your altar, or create a cornucopia to place them in. Include written messages that communicate your personal wishes for abundance and prosperity. Sprinkle the messages throughout the contents of the cornucopia, or place them in an offering bowl on your altar. As the season progresses, use the items in the cornucopia to feed yourself and your family, and replace them as needed. It is important to continually use and add to the altar until after Samhain to show the cycle of giving and receiving. Also, sharing your items with someone less fortunate will help sustain and promote your own abundance and increase your prosperity.

Charlynn Walls

August 27
Saturday

4th ♋

Color of the day: Indigo
Incense of the day: Sandalwood

Sharpen Your Visualization Skills

Visualization is a major part of the magical process. This exercise will help improve your visualization abilities. You'll need to do this with a magical friend or coven member. Here's what you'll need: a book/story you haven't read, plain white paper, and drawing tools—these could be colored pencils, crayons, or markers. Sit comfortably and have your drawing materials in front of you. Have your friend read a short passage to you. The reader can't show you any pictures. As your friend reads, "see" images in your mind. Begin to draw whatever you see or feel. When the reader stops, continue drawing if you wish. It can be as simple or detailed as you want. There is no right or wrong way to do this. It's meant to strengthen your spellcasting skills. You can also reverse roles, and you can read to your friend.

James Kambos

 August 28
Sunday

4th ♋

Color of the day: Gold
Incense of the day: Frankincense

Yin-Yang Balance

Sunday is the day of the sun, and yet today the moon is in Cancer, a most lunar and watery sign. So balance out your solar-aligned busy-ness and externally expressed action with some lunar introspection, cleansing, and loving self-care.

First, lightly clean and organize your space to create a more yin atmosphere while positioning yourself for more efficient yang action. Next, draw a bath. Add a tablespoon of sea salt to represent the ocean and the moon, and a few drops of frankincense oil to represent the sun. Stir the water in a counterclockwise direction with your left hand (to activate the water with lunar energy) and then in a clockwise direction with your right hand (for solar energy). Also light one white and one yellow candle to represent the moon and sun, respectively. Soak for at least forty minutes, as you feel yourself establishing an ideal equilibrium.

Tess Whitehurst

August 29

Monday

4th ♋

☽ v/c 2:23 am

☽ → ♌ 4:11 am

Color of the day: Lavender
Incense of the day: Lily

Peridot Spell for Release

Peridot is the birthstone for the month of August. This stone's lesson is to let go of the people and situations that are no longer healthy for you. Look for low-grade peridot stones for this spell, or simply use any peridot jewelry that you own. Hold the stone in your hand and concentrate on letting go of old hurts, ideas, and negativity that are no longer necessary in your life. Just let them go and watch these old negative thoughts evaporate away into nothing. Now raise your personal energy up from your center and say:

Peridot has a beautiful hue of golden green,

Help me release all the baggage to which I cling.

Now it'll dissolve and vanish safely into thin air,

By the stone's magick, I release all worries and cares.

Ellen Dugan

August 30

Tuesday

4th ♌

Color of the day: Scarlet
Incense of the day: Geranium

healing in the Face of the Unknown

Today happens to be the International Day of the Disappeared. This peculiar-sounding day is actually an observance to acknowledge those who are imprisoned and held against their will at locations and under (often poor) conditions unknown to their loved ones. Today, set upon your altar an empty photo frame, perhaps with a sheet of blank white or black paper within it, to represent those whose condition, location, and life status are unknown. Place and light in front of it a single white candle of healing and memory. Additionally, you can add to this memorial fresh flowers of your choice to represent healing in the lives of all affected. Invoke and say a prayer to a compassionate and healing deity or spirit that you have a working relationship with, such as Archangel Michael or Raphael, the Celtic goddess Brigid, or perhaps the Buddhist goddess Tara. May all experience healing in the face of the unknown.

Blake Octavian Blair

August 31
Wednesday

4th ♌

☽ v/c 12:20 am

☽ → ♍ 11:22 am

Color of the day: White
Incense of the day: Honeysuckle

A Memory Spell

School has just started again for many people, and this spell will help you remember what you learn in order to succeed. Choose a book that contains passages you want to remember. This may be something pertaining to a subject being studied, or something that you want to put into practice in your daily life. Sit in a quiet place and read the passage out loud. Read it a second time, envisioning the words being recorded in your memory so that you can replay them again later. Read the passage a third time, this time hearing the words as if they were being played back to you. You can do this with any passage that you need to try to commit to memory. It may take some practice, but it does work.

Charlie Rainbow Wolf

September

September is the ninth month of the year. Its name is derived from the Latin word *septum*, which means "seventh," as it was the seventh month of the Roman calendar. Its astrological sign is Virgo the maiden (August 23–September 23), a mutable earth sign ruled by Mercury. September is the dreamy golden afternoon of the year. Summer thins away, but September is a treasure chest filled with bounty and color. Apples ripen in the orchards. Purple grapes are harvested, and yellow heads of goldenrod nod along the roadsides. At Mabon, we celebrate the autumn equinox, and the dual nature of life/death. Now we're reminded of the goddess Demeter, and how her period of mourning for her abducted daughter Persephone coincides with nature's decline. To honor Demeter, drape your altar with purple fabric, and upon it place one red apple. Meditate about what you have and what you wish for. Bury the apple as you visualize your wish coming true. By September's end, autumn's flame begins to burn. You can see it in the orange of the maples and in the purple wild asters. Golden September—it's a time to dream, and a time to make those dreams come true.

James Kambos

September 1

Thursday

4th ♏

New Moon 5:03 am

Color of the day: Purple
Incense of the day: Myrrh

Solar Eclipse

New Moon Solar Eclipse

Today we have a solar eclipse, which means the moon is new. While the eclipse will only be visible over the African continent, the energy is still around us waiting to be put to use. This is a unique magickal time, as spells cast during an eclipse have staying power until the next eclipse occurs. Now that summer is drawing to a close and fall is just around the corner, let's use this opportunity to gather in abundance.

For this spell, you can burn a white candle for the new moon and a gold candle to represent all the wealth of the harvest season that is upon us. Light the candles and repeat this charm:

The solar eclipse is a magickal day.

I conjure for abundance to come my way.

A white candle for the new moon and starts that are fresh,

Gold for abundant harvest, that my spell may be blessed.

As the sun and moon now meet in the sky,

Let my spirit soar and my magick fly!

Ellen Dugan

NOTES:

September 2

Friday

1st ♍

☽ v/c 6:13 pm

☽ → ♎ 8:55 pm

Color of the day: Rose
Incense of the day: Rose

Friendship Popcorn Spell

One of my favorite areas to work magick for on Friday is friendship. Both Friday and the utilitarian crop of corn are ruled by Venus. These connections allow for a delightfully fun and tasty magickal combination. Today, for family members, classmates, or coworkers, pop up a batch of popcorn and put it into small individual-size paper bags, then distribute among them. Attach a short note (it can be simple and the same note for each) telling them you appreciate their friendship and to enjoy this special treat! You can also draw covert or overt magickal symbols on the bag, such as a heart or healing hand. Just like corn, friendships grow when nurtured, and we know that magickally we get back from the universe what we put out into it. So get popping and nurture a few friendships today, and watch the results return to you over time.

Blake Octavian Blair

 September 3

Saturday

1st ♎

Color of the day: Brown
Incense of the day: Patchouli

Diana's Bow

Look up to the sky this evening in the east after the sun has set. Do you see that slim sliver of a moon? That is called Diana's Bow; it represents the moon goddess pulling back her bowstring, poised and ready to shoot an arrow into the heavens. Hold a silver coin in your hand, and gaze upon the crescent moon and make a wish to her:

Lady Diana, I tie my dreams onto your arrow, flying fast and true as the sparrow.

Focus your dreams upon the moon so that they may fly into the sky and manifest. Blow the moon goddess a kiss as thanks for hearing your request. The coin should be reserved to drop into the first donation box you see.

Mickie Mueller

♡ September 4
Sunday

1st ♎

☽ v/c 8:30 pm

Color of the day: Amber
Incense of the day: Almond

An Apple Love Spell

Apples have always been linked to love magic. Now they're in season, so it's the perfect time to perform this love charm. When you're alone, read the following words aloud, then follow the spell as written.

In the mist of a September morn,

The power of this spell shall be born.

Go to an orchard before frost has kissed the ground,

Or anywhere that apples may be found.

Select an apple colored fiery red.

This is the fruit that shall turn another's head.

Rub it with a crimson cloth until it shines.

Love will find you with perfect speed and perfect time.

Then late at night, during the midnight hour,

Speak a love charm or words of power.

Consume this enchanted apple, but save the seeds.

Now trust the Fates to bring you the love you need.

James Kambos

NOTES:

September 5
Monday

1st ♎

☽ → ♏ 8:38 am

Color of the day: Silver
Incense of the day: Narcissus

Labor Day

Banishing the Feelings of Stress

Chronic stress can be damaging to the body, but unfortunately many of us have highly stressful lives. A quick method of grounding stressful energy is to use a meditation such as the following.

Close your eyes and imagine a pillar of white light shining down upon you, the energy going through you and down deep into the earth. Focus on your breath. As you breathe in, more of the light pours down on you, and when you breathe out, the energy moves through you, carrying any tension, stress, or discomfort out of you and down into the earth to be recycled. After a few minutes, when you feel better, allow the energy to cease, with the intention of keeping only what you need and releasing the rest into the earth. Open your eyes.

Since this meditation is quick, it can be repeated often as needed.

Michael Furie

September 6
Tuesday

1st ♏

Color of the day: Red
Incense of the day: Basil

Spell for Embarking on a New Study Topic

This is the season we associate with "back to school," and it's a perfect time to begin a new course of magical study. You may decide to read up on a new subject (such as herbalism or tarot) or learn a new magic-related skill (like calligraphy or drumming).

Gather the tools of your new discipline (books, materials, instruments, etc.) and place them on or near your altar. Today, a Tuesday, is aligned with the god Mars, a deity associated with fire, passion, initiative, and war. The passion of Mars can be used for positive energy, especially in matters where courage and passion come into play. Light a candle and do a blessing, invoking the names of gods associated with fire energy: Mars, Ares, Vulcan, Apollo (a solar god). Invoke their names to bless your new study venture. For example, you might say:

Gods of fire: Mars, Ares, Vulcan, Apollo! Awaken in me the heat of intelligence, passion, and will. Light the flames of inspiration and courage within me. So mote it be!

Peg Aloi

September 7
Wednesday

1st ♏

☽ v/c 8:43 pm

☽ → ♐ 9:20 pm

Color of the day: Yellow
Incense of the day: Marjoram

Mercury Retrograde Magic

Wednesday is ruled by Mercury, and (as you may know) Mercury is currently retrograde. While Mercury retrograde periods may not be ideal for making decisions or purchases, or entering into new agreements or undertakings, they are ideal for tying up loose ends by revisiting old goals, finishing projects, and untangling any less than stellar communications. So today, burn sandalwood incense, grab a notebook, and brainstorm a list of any loose ends that you might benefit from tying up. Write down anything you can think of, and then narrow it down to things on which you may actually be able to make progress. Take time with each item, brainstorming untried strategies for moving forward in each area. Finish by smudging your journal and yourself with the sandalwood as you chant:

My road is open and my way is clear.

Vow to take action on your list before the full moon on the 17th.

Tess Whitehurst

September 8
Thursday

1st ♐

Color of the day: Turquoise
Incense of the day: Jasmine

An Ointment to Take You in the Right Direction

For this spell, you'll need about ¼ cup coconut oil, a shaving of beeswax, three drops peppermint oil, a small ramekin dish, and a small wide-mouthed jar or bottle. Put the coconut oil and beeswax in the ramekin. Place this in a pan of hot water, taking care that the water does not simmer into the ramekin. When the coconut oil and beeswax have melted, remove from the heat and allow to cool, stirring a couple times. As the mixture starts to set, add the peppermint oil. Place in the jar to cool thoroughly. Rub this on the soles of your feet for a month in order to help you find direction and purpose in your life.

Charlie Rainbow Wolf

September 9
Friday

1st ♐
2nd Quarter 7:49 am
☽ v/c 8:51 pm

Color of the day: White
Incense of the day: Cypress

Blessing Jar Spell

Using a clear jar that you find pleasing, and stones, crystals, shells, beads, coins, old jewelry, or charms, focus on the symbolism of these items and the blessings you wish to bring into your life you add each item of your choosing to the jar. Then pour a small handful of clean sand (you can wash natural sand, or purchase decorative sand from a craft store) on top of the items, to ground them in earth and the energies of manifestation. Then pour water over all as you think of your gratitude for all that you currently have in your life. Shake the jar gently to see how things might "shake out" in your life, and let it settle. Store the jar on your altar where you can see it every day, to remind you of your gratitude for all you have, as well as what's now manifesting in your life.

Thuri Calafia

September 10
Saturday

2nd ♐
☽ → ♑ 8:55 am

Color of the day: Blue
Incense of the day: Sage

A Request for the Queen of Vodou

Legend has it that if you want a wish fulfilled, visit the grave of Vodou priestess Marie Laveau in New Orleans. Knock three times, speak your desire, then mark three Xs on the tomb to seal the deal. (Don't actually try this, though—it's illegal.)

Invoke the power of the Vodou Queen with a petition candle. Carve three large Xs into a white candle while reciting your request aloud. Dress the candle with Van Van oil, then rub black glitter and crushed chili pepper (for fidelity and to "heat things up") into your carving. Light the candle, repeating your petition one last time.

Let the candle burn down completely. Scrape any remaining wax, pepper, and glitter out of the holder, and bury the lot with these words:

Thank you, Mama Marie,
for your intercession.

When your desire comes to pass, leave a coin where you buried the wax.

Natalie Zaman

September 11

Sunday

2nd ♑

Color of the day: Yellow
Incense of the day: Heliotrope

A New Day of Thanks

A day filled with tragedy often makes us forget to feel gratitude for what we have. Appreciating our loved ones while they're still here with us is one of the most important aspects of life. Take some time to remind yourself of the abundance and happiness in your life.

Find a comfortable place to sit, outdoors if possible. Write down all of the positives in your life. What do you have to be thankful for? Your friends? Family? Career? Delve into the different aspects of your life, and think about all of the things you have been blessed with. Once you get going, you may find it hard to stop! Take as much time and paper as you need. When you're done, thank your deities for these gifts. Keep your list in a handy location to remind you of your blessings when you need it.

Kerri Connor

 September 12

Monday

2nd ♑

☽ v/c 6:00 am

☽ → ♒ 5:28 pm

Color of the day: White
Incense of the day: Rosemary

Cauldron of Cerridwen

Cerridwen is the Welsh goddess of magic and transformation. She is associated with the cauldron of Awen, from which wisdom springs forth. Invoke Cerridwen when you need a boost to inspire you. Here is an invocation that works well:

Cerridwen, who is the keeper of the cauldron,

The wellspring of inspiration,

Bestow transformative powers upon my mind.

Let me be open to all that is possible.

May the ideas flow forth

And be tempered with your wisdom.

As I will, so shall it be!

Charlynn Walls

September 13
Tuesday

2nd ≈≈

Color of the day: Black
Incense of the day: Ylang-ylang

Pop-Culture Confidence

We all have times when we need a boost of self-confidence. Maybe you're about to ask your boss for a raise or finally ask out that cute coworker. Either way, making a good impression and being self-confident are paramount.

Think of your favorite characters from pop culture. Pick a character who best embodies the characteristics that you want to convey. To impress a coworker with your knowledge, you might choose Hermione Granger. To show your boss your business savvy, you might choose Bruce Wayne. To show your empathy and loyalty, you might choose Samwise Gamgee.

Envision that character standing behind you and then stepping into your body, imbuing you with his or her positive characteristics. Then go do what you need to do with the full confidence that you have the energy of that character riding within you. Once you've finished, envision that character stepping back out of you and receding back into the ether.

Emily Carlin

NOTES:

September 14

Wednesday

2nd ♒

☽ v/c 11:31 am

☽ → ♓ 10:23 pm

Color of the day: Topaz
Incense of the day: Lavender

hearth Blessing

It's the season of returning indoors, putting bare feet back into shoes, hanging up bathing suits, and putting on clothes. Kids return to school, and adults return to work and routines.

Transitioning indoors, bless your home and hearth. Scatter a pinch of salt in front of each of your entrances, opening the doors wide, saying:

Goddesses bless this home and all who enter. Protect the people, spirits, and place.

Light a sage stick. Walk through each room, fanning the smoke:

Gods cleanse this home, purify and bless. May only good spirits dwell here.

At the heart of the home (you decide where that is), smudge carefully:

Goddesses and Gods reside here. Protect, love, nurture, and guide here.

Extinguish the sage, and carefully go to close all the doors. As doors close, know that your hearth is blessed, ready for the indoor season:

We're blessed and protected inside our home.

Dallas Jennifer Cobb

Notes:

September 15
Thursday

2nd ♓

Color of the day: Crimson
Incense of the day: Carnation

Money-Drawing Oil

Creating this oil on a Thursday right before the full moon will add to this already powerful money-drawing oil recipe. You'll need a small bottle to keep your oil in. Make sure you label it. Here are the ingredients:

- 2 parts jojoba oil or olive oil
- 1 part bergamot oil
- 1 part patchouli oil
- A few flakes of basil
- A clove
- Iron filings
- Lodestone or a small piece of magnet

After mixing your oil, hold it in your hands and visualize golden light flowing into the oil from all directions. Fill the oil with your intention that it will become a money magnet that will draw prosperity into your life. Use it to anoint the corners of your wallet, prosperity candles, your credit or debit cards, and cash before you spend it, to ensure that energetically it will return to you. A little of this oil goes a long way.

Mickie Mueller

 ## September 16
Friday

2nd ♓

☽ v/c 3:05 pm

Full Moon 3:05 pm

Color of the day: Coral
Incense of the day: Violet

Lunar Eclipse

Activate Psychic Abilities

A lunar eclipse is like an extra-strength full moon, during which your emotions might run high and a sort of swirling, spiraling dreaminess may seem to supersede your everyday linear awareness. On top of all of this, today's full moon is in Pisces, the sign of feelings, intuition, and fluid depths. So if there was ever a night to activate your psychic abilities, this is it! Alone or with a like-minded friend or group, visit a clean natural body of water under the full moon. Alternatively, visit a pool or hot tub, or even draw a bath. Begin to align your personal energy with the energy of the water and the moon as you chant:

Flowing water, ocean deep,

Into your fluid realm I leap.

Great power to see, great power to heal,

I receive now as to you I yield.

Then immerse yourself completely in the water.

Tess Whitehurst

September 17
Saturday

3rd ♈

☽ → ♈ 12:22 am

Color of the day: Gray
Incense of the day: Pine

Bless the herbs

Garden herbs aren't just for flavoring foods. Herbs are sacred plants that contain magical and healing properties. So at this time of year, as you harvest your herbs to dry for winter use, do so with magical intent. Herbs are sensitive to our personal energy. This blessing ritual will charge your herbs with extra power for magical or culinary purposes. Say the blessing:

Now the wild geese are flying,

And the grasses of the fields are dying.

But before my garden turns to rust,

And before the flowers fall to dust,

Thank you, Divine Power, for these sacred herbs.

As I bless them with my words—

Noble plants that heal me,

Noble plants that feed me,

Noble plants that work magic for me—

I honor you. Blessed be!

After the herbs dry, scatter a few in your garden as an offering.

James Kambos

September 18
Sunday

3rd ♈

☽ v/c 4:11 pm

Color of the day: Gold
Incense of the day: Hyacinth

Celebrating Individuality and Uniqueness

Famed musical artist and guitarist Jimi Hendrix passed away on this date in 1970. Hendrix was known for his unique sound and playing style. He was unafraid to push the envelope of accepted norms and boundaries of traditional musical genres. All of us have experienced others imposing their definitions of how things should be and perceptions of "the norm" upon our creative outlets or our individuality of how we choose to express ourselves. Today is a day to remember that, as long as we aren't hurting anyone or ourselves, it's okay to push these creative envelopes! Today, engage in the creative expression of your choice and share it with others who appreciate your talents and unique flair. This in turn will pass on the inspiration of uniqueness. Creation is an act of magick: share an original poem, go dancing, make music, paint! By celebrating your uniqueness, you also honor those qualities in others.

Blake Octavian Blair

September 19

Monday

3rd ♉

☽ → ♉ 12:58 am

Color of the day: Gray
Incense of the day: Neroli

Spell to Find a Lost Item

Avast, me hearties! It's International Talk Like a Pirate Day! There is a spell that I've had requests for repeatedly over the years, and that is my spell to find a lost item. This little gem is simple and works every time!

To begin, visualize the item that is lost. Now in your mind's eye, encircle it with a silver cord. Now tug the cord back toward your solar plexus. See the lost item being pulled back to you. While doing so, repeat this charm three times:

What was lost now is found,

As my magick circles round.

Whether you are hidden far or near,

I call you now to come meet me here.

This spell works for cellphones, tablets, jewelry, keys, paperwork…you get the idea. If you choose to tart it up today and talk like a pirate—well, go for it!

Ellen Dugan

September 20

Tuesday

3rd ♉

☽ v/c 11:32 pm

Color of the day: Maroon
Incense of the day: Ginger

Spell for Welcoming Autumn

The autumnal equinox is a potent time occurring at a precise astrological moment, but the period leading up to autumn is more of a mood shift that many of us feel deeply, especially in the Northeast, where the visual changes are dramatic. The cooler temperatures and decreasing daylight also mark a shift in energy. This can be a very creative time, so harness that creativity to bring you into the winter season. To welcome this energy, turn your altar into an autumn landscape. Place acorns, apples, colorful autumn leaves, pine cones, and other natural objects over autumn-colored fabrics. Add candles, herbs, and gemstones appropriate to the season. Each night, light the candles and acknowledge the decreasing daylight, saying:

As daylight wanes, the colors increase;
as the leaves fall, my creativity blooms.

Add natural objects to your altar as the season progresses, and get out for walks each day to observe the changes.

Peg Aloi

September 21
Wednesday

3rd ♉

☽ → ♊ 1:53 am

Color of the day: White
Incense of the day: Bay laurel

UN International Day of Peace

A Silent Prayer for Peace

Today is the International Day of Peace. To observe this important holiday, get a tealight candle and carve a number of peace signs on its surface. Anoint the candle with an essential oil of your choice, something that represents peace and healing. Visualize the candle surrounded in a vibrant blue glow. If you wish, put on some meditative, peaceful music that aligns your mind with calm thoughts. Engage in deep breathing and slow your movements.

After you light the candle, look at a globe or a world map (even if it's on the computer) and make clockwise circular movements with the flame in front of every continent, island, country, and body of water. Take some time with this remote blessing, encompassing every area of the world.

Visualize peaceful, loving energies positively connecting everyone and everything on the planet as you carefully allow the candle to burn to its end.

Raven Digitalis

 ## September 22
Thursday

3rd ♊

☉ → ♎ 10:21 am

Color of the day: Green
Incense of the day: Balsam

Mabon – Fall Equinox

A Spell to Find Balance

This is the day when daytime and nighttime are of equal proportions. It is a wonderful opportunity to bring yourself into balance and harmony, too. You'll need a stone about the size of your fist and some time to go on a long walk, preferably by water. As you commence your journey, start talking to the stone. You may feel silly, but if you can speak out loud, it's even more powerful. Tell the stone all your troubles and hangups, everything that is stealing away your centeredness. When you've said all you have to say, throw the stone far away, into the water if possible. Don't even watch it land; just throw it, and know that you have thrown all your obstacles away with it. Return home and take a nice relaxing bath to complete the cleansing.

Charlie Rainbow Wolf

September 23

Friday

3rd ♊

☽ v/c 3:57 am

☽ → ♋ 4:33 am

4th Quarter 5:56 am

Color of the day: Rose
Incense of the day: Thyme

Protection Spice Herb Blend

Here is a formula for a magical blend that offers protective energies to the one who consumes it. This mixture can be a seasoning added to food as a way to bring personal protection to one person or an entire group. It's a quick bit of kitchen witchery. Combine two tablespoons each of dried basil and oregano with a half teaspoon each of granulated onion, granulated or powdered garlic, and sea salt in a bowl, and stir with your fingers to mix. As you stir the ingredients, empower them with protection energy and say:

Herbs of the earth and salt of the sea,
those who partake shall blessed be;
safe and secure, protected and well,
charged with intent by magic spell.

Pour the herbs into a bottle and use as desired.

Michael Furie

September 24

Saturday

4th ♋

☽ v/c 9:42 pm

Color of the day: Black
Incense of the day: Ivy

Cutting the Ties That Bind

We all find ourselves with extra baggage from expired relationships. Take a moment to tap into the energies of the planet Saturn and banish the unneeded or unwanted. Take a length of gray cord to represent the muddled emotions that are still tying you to the person. Then take a pair of scissors and cut the cord in half while saying:

I remove this person and his/her
energy from my life.

Repeat with each remaining half until only the smallest parts remain. The remaining pieces of the cord can then be buried so that the relationship can be mourned.

Charlynn Walls

September 25

Sunday

4th ♋

☽ → ♌ 9:48 am

Color of the day: Orange
Incense of the day: Eucalyptus

Sacred Siblings

B orn to the same parents and given similar early-life experiences, our siblings are bound to us in a complicated and complex manner. Today, celebrate the sacredness of sibling bonds, knowing that whether we love, like, are indifferent to, or disdain them, our siblings are part of our sacred path.

Gather a picture of your siblings, or an item that he or she touched, and do a small blessing ritual. If you don't have "born" siblings, celebrate your "chosen" siblings. Say:

My brother/sister, I honor you and bless your strong spirit.

My brother/sister, I respect you and bless your distinct life path.

My brother/sister, I know you and bless our shared origins.

My brother/sister, I bless you and wish you ongoing health and healing.

May you journey wisely on your sacred path, and walk with the Gods and Goddesses.

Blessed be, sacred sibling(s).

Dallas Jennifer Cobb

September 26

Monday

4th ♌

Color of the day: Silver
Incense of the day: Narcissus

A Breath of Fresh Air

S pring cleaning is a chance to open the windows and give your house a good cleaning after the long winter while letting fresh air and sunshine into your home. Why not add a special fall cleaning to your projects to give yourself a good cleaning and to let in some fresh air and sunshine while it is still around to be had? After all, a good cleansing should take place more than just once a year. Use a natural cleaner, such as lemon or cinnamon oil with vinegar water, to scrub down walls, cupboards, and windows. (I use one cup of vinegar to a gallon of water and fifteen drops of oil.) Breathe in the scent as you work for your own personal cleansing. As you clean, focus on clearing the space of negative energy along with dirt buildup. When you're done, keep the windows open while you do an intense smudging. Allow the air to carry the smoke throughout your home.

Kerri Connor

September 27

Tuesday

4th ♌

☽ v/c 4:52 am

☽ → ♍ 5:43 pm

Color of the day: White

Incense of the day: Cedar

Spell to Reap Your Inner Harvest

Today's moon is what I like to call a Crone's sickle—three days until she's new, the moon can be seen like a luminous scythe—for cutting old ties or culling a garden. At this time of year, we harvest many things, from balcony gardens to huge fields, from major life events to seemingly tiny changes that can have great effects later on.

What still needs harvesting in your inner landscape? What have you planted, nurtured, and worked so hard for, and are now anticipating with excitement or even frustration? Get those energies moving by placing a dish of soil on your altar and placing a red votive or tealight candle in the center of the soil. Say:

As the moon wanes, as the year wanes, so let my efforts be reaped. As the candle glows, as the sun god goes, let the mother bring forth what I seek!

Repeat the chant nine times, ending with:

So mote it be!

Thuri Calafia

 September 28

Wednesday

4th ♍

Color of the day: Brown

Incense of the day: Lilac

Elemental Centering

Here is a short ritual you can do anytime to give your magick a boost.

Visualize the four elements around you, with you as the center.

In your mind's eye, feel the power of the north, the power of earth, flow through you, growing up from the ground and bringing you strength, stability, and grounding.

Feel the power of the east, the power of air, flow through you like wind, bringing you wisdom, communication, and inspiration.

Feel the power of the south, the power of fire, burn through you, bringing you passion, will, and true power.

Feel the power of the west, the power of water, flow through you, bringing you purity, healing, and rebirth.

Feel the elements dancing within you. Feel your spirit uniting with them, binding them together, uniting them within you. You are flooded with the full power of nature.

Emily Carlin

September 29

Thursday

4th ♏

☽ v/c 6:05 am

Color of the day: White
Incense of the day: Mulberry

Invoking Saint Michael

Blessed Michaelmas! Today we honor the warrior archangel who led the divine army against the forces of evil. Call Michael's spirit to your side by creating a special altar to him. Arrange nine blue candles in a circle on your altar (nine for Michael's month, and blue, Michael's color). If you have a statue or picture of Michael, or a devotional candle with his image on it, set it in the center of the circle. Place peppers, cinnamon, cumin, or other hot foods and spices in the circle as well. Michael is associated with the sun, so hot foods are appropriate offerings to him. Light the candles with these words:

Warrior and angel,

Lend me your sword, Michael.

Guard me, guide me, and stay by my side.

Invoke Michael's spirit whenever you need a warrior presence in your life.

Natalie Zaman

September 30

Friday

4th ♏

☽ → ♎ 3:52 am

New Moon 8:11 pm

Color of the day: Purple
Incense of the day: Cypress

A New Moon Spell for Increasing Awareness

Witchcraft and magick are both practices and philosophies that rely on healthy levels of self-awareness. When we can see our own intentions and motivations clearly, we can more easily perceive those of other people. This, in turn, increases objective psychic awareness and empathic discretion.

To help increase self-awareness, situate yourself in a ritual space. Perform a new moon esbat ceremony. If you are new to practicing the Craft, simply research various methods in books that explore the mysteries of the dark moon.

At the height of your personal ceremony, put some red sandalwood powder in a dish and mix it into a paste using water or mineral oil. Apply this to your Ajna chakra (brow), and visualize your third-eye chakra growing with awareness while the moon begins its waxing cycle.

Raven Digitalis

October

October is a busy month. Originally the eighth month of the year (*octo* being eight) in the Roman calendar, it was set back to the tenth month around 700 BCE, when King Numa Pompilius revised the calendar and added January and February.

The ancient Egyptians celebrate the Festival of Het-Hert, or Hathor, on October 4th. The Romans celebrate Meditrinalia on October 11th, tasting the new wine for the first time and honoring Jupiter as god of the wine. And the Celts close out their year at Samhain on October 31st.

In October, we are most aware of the shortening of the days, the cooling weather, the changing colors of the trees and the falling of the leaves, glowing fires, orange pumpkins, and warm scarves and mittens.

The last of the harvest festivals arrives at Halloween. The veil thins, and we feel the presence of our ancestors and those we cherish who have passed over. We set a place at the table for them and celebrate with them the passing of another season and the closing of another year.

The larders are full against the coming winter months. The last mornings of October bring the killing frosts, and we wait prepared for the change in season yet to come.

Boudica

October 1

Saturday

1st ♎

Color of the day: Gray
Incense of the day: Sage

The Check's in the Mail Spell

We've all heard the saying "The check's in the mail." Well, how about sending yourself a check for a change? The idea of this spell is that you'll be drawing money to you. Here's what to do. Light an orange or gold candle. Sit before the candle with one of your blank checks. Think of a realistic amount of money you'd like to have, and make out the check, payable to you, for that amount. Rub the check with a lucky stone such as a citrine. Send it. When the check comes back to you, open the envelope and lay the check on your altar. For three nights, light the same candle you used earlier. Then hide the check and try to forget about it. When the spell works for you, donate a small amount to a charity.

James Kambos

October 2

Sunday

1st ♎

☽ v/c 1:43 am
☽ → ♏ 3:43 pm

Color of the day: Gold
Incense of the day: Marigold

Marjoram for Mehr

Today is Mehrgan, the Persian festival of autumn that honors the goddess Mehr, the spirit of love, friendship, and commitments. Altars to Mehr are decorated in bright colors and include bunches of dried marjoram, an herb associated with Venus and Aphrodite and often used in happiness and love charms.

To honor Mehr and ensure happiness in the coming year, fashion a poppet of her to keep in your home. Wash and dry a generous bunch of fresh marjoram. Form a head, arms, and body by tying off sections with brightly colored thread. As you craft the poppet, invoke the goddess's spirit:

Sweet Lady Mehr, bless us with your loving kindness.

Bring happiness and plenty to our home.

Hang the poppet where your family congregates for meals. When the marjoram has dried completely, use it to infuse soups and other comforting recipes with Mehr's autumnal magic.

Natalie Zaman

NOTES:

 October 3

Monday

1st ♏

Color of the day: Lavender
Incense of the day: Rosemary

Rosh hashanah

Moon Day Advice

Monday's planetary ruler is the Moon. For many people, Monday is the start of the work week and can be a rough day. However, things always go better if we have a game plan. Gather a small piece of moonstone and your favorite tarot deck. Pull the Moon card and lay the moonstone on top of it. Next pull three additional cards, to represent your morning, afternoon, and night. Lay them below the Moon card. Analyze the cards and, based on the information they tell you, formulate a game plan for going about your day. Now that you have a forecast, you can dress for the weather, so to speak! Carry the moonstone with you in a small bag or in your pocket. As the day's events unfold, it will remind you that you have a plan for handling them.

Blake Octavian Blair

October 4
Tuesday

1st ♏

☽ v/c 9:04 pm

Color of the day: Black
Incense of the day: Bayberry

Animal Blessing

It's World Animal Day and Saint Francis of Assisi's feast day. Find, create, or print out an image of Saint Francis, and glue or otherwise attach it to a tall, white devotional jar candle. Hold the candle in both hands and say:

> Saint Francis, please bless the animals in my life (or home). May they be happy, may they be healthy, may they be safe. Also bless all the animals in the world: surround them in kindness, comfort, and love. Open my heart and the hearts of other humans fully to other species, so that we may not harm them or use them, but rather respect and treasure them as brothers and sisters in Gaia. Thank you.

Visualize bright pinkish-white light emanating from your heart, moving down your arms, and filling the candle. Light the candle and visualize this light spreading to the hearts of all animals (humans and otherwise) on the planet.

Tess Whitehurst

October 5
Wednesday

1st ♏

☽ → ♐ 4:26 am

Color of the day: White
Incense of the day: Lilac

Autumn Leaf Spell for Releasing Obstacles

This time of year is ideal for dissolution and release. For this spell, gather some large dried leaves, one for each obstacle you'd like to release (five or less is best). Using either a felt pen, ink, or paint, write one specific thing you wish to be released from your life on each leaf. Remember, for banishings there is a need to be specific; a general "banish all my obstacles" can result in having things or people removed from your life that you'd rather keep. Once you figure out exactly what you wish to be released and have written it on the leaves, hold each leaf, charging it with the desire to be free from that obstacle. In the flame of a black candle, light each leaf and drop it into a cauldron to burn out. This is best done outdoors or on the stove with the hood fan on to remove the smoke.

Michael Furie

·October 6
Thursday

1st ♐

Color of the day: Green
Incense of the day: Nutmeg

A Spell to Build Your Book of Shadows

This waxing-moon phase is the time to work magick and to add to the pages of your grimoire or personal book of shadows. Set the book up on your work space, and surround it with simple white tealights. Now light the candles one at a time, going in a clockwise direction. Hold your hands up and toward the book but safely away from the candles. Say:

As the moon does grow fuller and fuller each night,

My book of shadows grows too, in knowledge and light.

A place for charms, and spells, and magickal things,

I enchant this book inside a candle ring.

By earth, air, sky, and sea, as above now so below,

The elemental powers spin and my magick holds.

Ellen Dugan

 ·October 7
Friday

1st ♐

☽ v/c 2:26 am

☽ → ♑ 4:40 pm

Color of the day: White
Incense of the day: Orchid

A New Friend Spell

This time of year, many people start to feel the winter blues approaching. You may be a bit nostalgic about the summer fun or apprehensive about the coming winter. This spell will help to beat those blues and banish any loneliness that you may be feeling. You will need some catnip or catmint, a pink candle, and a pen and paper. Make a tea out of the catnip by pouring hot water on it, then straining it into a cup. Light the pink candle. On the piece of paper, write, "Friend, come and find me." Sip the cup of tea, projecting your thoughts of love and friendship into the universe. When the tea is finished, carefully burn the paper in the candle and snuff it out. Now find a new activity or hobby, and know that you will find new friends, too.

Charlie Rainbow Wolf

October 8

Saturday

1st ℣

Color of the day: Black
Incense of the day: Sandalwood

Relationship Evaluations

As we head into the dark half of the year, many people are turning their workings inward. One way to do this is to take a look at your relationships—all of them, not just romantic ones—and see how things are working for you. Do you have some relationships that could be described as rocky at best? What do you put into these relationships, and what do you get out of them? Are they one-sided? Is it in your best interest to continue these relationships? Take a relaxing, cleansing bath, adding a few drops of frankincense and myrrh oils to the water. Mentally list the pros and cons of each questionable relationship. Can a relationship be saved? Work on it. Is a relationship beyond salvation or repair? Say goodbye with this cleansing bath and then say goodbye in person as well. Don't feel guilty about thinking of yourself; bad relationships can be destructive. End them before they get to that point.

Kerri Connor

October 9

Sunday

1st ℣
2nd Quarter 12:33 am
☽ v/c 12:51 pm

Color of the day: Amber
Incense of the day: Juniper

Honoring the Traveler

Today is the official observance of Leif Erikson Day in honor of his discovery of America. In honor of discovery and exploration, take a little time to explore a part of your area that you are unfamiliar with. You could take a drive in the country, or, if you're feeling more adventurous, take a tour of a cave or other landmark near you. Be bold and get out of your comfort zone today. Once you get home, light a candle to remember a fellow traveler. Reflect on what you've experienced and offer thanks.

Charlynn Walls

·October 10

Monday

2nd ♑

☽ → ♒ 2:33 am

Color of the day: Ivory
Incense of the day: Hyssop

Columbus Day (observed)

Spell to Bless Shrines for the Dead

It's appropriate, as Samhain approaches, to honor our beloved dead by building small shrines to their memory. Any small space will do: a section of the mantle, a bookshelf or bookcase top or end, a wall niche, or even a TV tray set up for the purpose. Place a fabric scrap or a scarf over the area, and decorate the space with mementos of each of your honored dead. You can even place a small offering dish, if you would like to leave offerings to the spirits. Finally, place a tealight candle in a holder in the center of the space and anoint it with oil, imagining the spirit of your loved one in the candle.

As you light the candle, say these or similar words:

> Spirit of _____ , I welcome you
> here to commune with me and to
> receive my love. Blessed be.

Take some time and speak to the spirit of your loved one, sharing memories and blessings. Repeat the candle lighting nightly, if you wish, throughout the holiday season.

Thuri Calafia

Notes:

October 11

Tuesday

2nd ♒

☽ v/c 7:49 pm

Color of the day: Gray
Incense of the day: Cinnamon

Walking Your Own Path

Sometimes we find ourselves at a crossroads in our lives, and it's difficult to know what choice to make. This simple meditation can help you decide.

Sit comfortably and close your eyes. Envision yourself walking down a path. The path is a little rough and uneven, but nothing you can't handle. Eventually you stop as you come to a crossroads. From here, each path leads into a small clearing, just out of sight. These paths are your choices. Take a moment and walk each path to see where it leads. As you walk these paths, you see the potential outcomes for the choices you might make. Once you have walked all the paths, return to the crossroads. Feel the energy of the various paths. Does a particular path pull you more than the others? Choose the path that showed you the outcome you most favor and that pulled you the strongest. When you're ready, open your eyes.

Emily Carlin

 October 12

Wednesday

2nd ♒

☽ → ♓ 8:43 am

Color of the day: Yellow
Incense of the day: Honeysuckle

Yom Kippur

Feet in the Soil

This unique working makes use of the Witch's famous conical hat. If you don't own one, feel free to buy a pointy hat that calls to you (they're readily available at this time of year).

In the dead of night, put on some comfortable black clothing and journey to a natural, quiet outdoor location where you won't be disturbed. Bring with you two large tree branches that you have discovered fallen in nature. Also bring a little spade or garden shovel, as well as a folding chair.

When you arrive in your chosen spot, dig a hole in the soil and cover your feet. Wear your conical hat and, sitting in the chair, hold the branches high above you, with one in each hand.

Feel yourself "becoming" a tree. Contemplate the cycle of carbon and oxygen, photosynthesis, and the life cycle of the tree. Visualize the power entering you through the branches, your feet, and the conical hat. When you feel deeply grounded and connected, disassemble the scene and note any mystical sensations.

Raven Digitalis

NOTES:

October 13
Thursday

2nd ♓

Color of the day: Purple
Incense of the day: Clove

Wish Upon a Star

What is your greatest wish? Head outside at night under the stars, and write down your wish on a piece of paper. Be as specific as possible, including as many details as you can. Then dig a small hole in the ground or use a fireproof container, and light the paper. Allow it to burn, letting the smoke release your wish into the universe. As the paper burns, look up into the sky and pick out the first star you see. Remember this childhood rhyme?

> Star light, star bright,
>
> First star I see tonight,
>
> I wish I may, I wish I might,
>
> Have this wish I wish tonight.

Chant this over and over as your paper burns, releasing your magic into the night air.

Kerri Connor

October 14

Friday

2nd ♓

☽ v/c 3:13 am

☽ → ♈ 11:08 am

Color of the day: Pink
Incense of the day: Alder

Falling Leaf Spell

According to tree lore, if you can snatch a leaf blown from a tree in midair before it hits the ground, it will be a good-luck talisman for the coming year. Call to the tree or trees of your choice:

I celebrate your falling leaves as you cycle throughout the year,

I wish to catch one in my hand, I request with love and good cheer!

You'll have to be quick of eye and fleet of foot to position yourself under a falling leaf. I tried this with my four oak trees, and it took me about a half hour, but I did finally get one. When you finally catch one, it's so exciting! Be sure to thank the tree, and find a place to keep your lucky leaf where it won't get damaged or lost. You could even place it in a small frame and hang it on the wall as art.

Mickie Mueller

October 15

Saturday

2nd ♈

Color of the day: Blue
Incense of the day: Magnolia

Crystal Grid for the home

We all strive to make our home a cozy and energetically welcoming place for ourselves and our loved ones. This requires a bit of spiritual and magickal upkeep. Tonight's full moon (it's full tomorrow morning, technically) is perfect for manifestation magick, and a simple crystal grid is a great way to keep good vibes flowing. Gather four quartz-crystal points of any size and a fifth crystal of any type, chosen depending upon the energies you'd like to impart throughout your home. This fifth stone will be the center of your grid. Cleanse your crystals, then arrange them on your altar or a central location. Place your fifth stone (chosen for its properties) in the center, with the four points arranged around it, pointing toward the four corners of your home. Hold your hands over the grid and focus on the intent of your goal, then charge the grid with the purpose of constantly sending those energies throughout your dwelling.

Blake Octavian Blair

October 16

Sunday

2nd ♈

☽ v/c 12:23 am

Full Moon 12:23 am

☽ → ♉ 11:04 am

Color of the day: Orange

Incense of the day: Almond

Apple Spell for Wisdom

This is the height of apple harvest season. If you don't live in an area with orchards where you can pick them, pick some up at a farm stand or grocery store. Get seven apples, one for each day of the week, and place them on your altar. Each morning, before breakfast, take one apple and cut through it in the middle, sideways, so that each half is round, the top and the bottom of the apple. In the middle of each half you will see a pentacle shape made by the seeds: the apple's magic lies within but is also throughout, given its sweetness, fragrance, beauty, and folklore. Look at the halved apple for a few minutes, meditating on the meaning of the pentacle (the elements, wholeness, integration). Then eat the apple, savoring its flavor and visualizing its wisdom and health-giving properties. Do this each day for a week.

Peg Aloi

▽ **October 17**

Monday

3rd ♉

☽ v/c 10:47 am

Color of the day: Silver

Incense of the day: Clary sage

Sukkot begins

A Dirty Little Secret Spell

It happens now and then. You learn about somebody's dirty little secret. So let's say you find out that nice man across the street—the perfect family man—is having an affair, which explains all those "business" trips to Des Moines. What do you do? You could blab it all over the block and become known as the neighborhood gossip. Or you could perform this spell. Let's go for the spell.

You'll need paper, pen, soil, and a jar with a lid. First write the secret on the paper without using names. Fold the paper and place in the jar. Now fill the jar with soil and screw on the lid. Bury the jar away from your property and say:

The dirty secret I hold

Shall never be told.

I will never utter a sound.

Let it lie buried in the ground.

James Kambos

October 18

Tuesday

3rd ♉

☽ → ♊ 10:30 am

Color of the day: Maroon
Incense of the day: Cedar

Spell to Succeed in School

Buy some yellow beeswax sheets and roll a thick pillar candle in which you've sprinkled rose oil and very lightly sprinkled rosemary and sage (you don't want the herbs to catch fire—I speak from experience!), or make an oil of the herbs (sunflower or almond oil is a good base) and add the rose oil for anointing a purchased yellow pillar.

First, you may wish to carve the purchased candle, or do cutouts or add-ons on the last layer of the beeswax candle with symbols of wisdom and mental power. Just for fun, sprinkle the candle with yellow or gold glitter, to remind you of the sun god and/or sparks of illumination. Then hold the candle in your hands and say:

I'm smart and wise, and I remember
ALL that I learn!

Anoint the candle from the top down, to pull in energy. Light the candle every time you study. For an added boost on test days, you may want to use some of the oil on *yourself*. Best of luck in school!

Thuri Calafia

 October 19

Wednesday

3rd ♊

Color of the day: Brown
Incense of the day: Lavender

Memento Mori Meditation

The skull is symbolic of our shared condition; it is the casing of the brain, the mortal shell that houses the immortal soul. Replicas and images of human skulls are meditative tools that can help us connect to the spirit world, and they are plentiful in many shops at this time of year.

Place a model or image of a skull at your bedside, along with your book of shadows or a journal. Before you sleep, ground and center, then gaze into the skull's eyes and speak this gravestone incantation:

Look into my eyes and know,

Beyond this world we all must go.

Whisper now from where you be,

What messages do you have for me?

Record any dreams or visions that come to you in the night. Did you make a connection?

Natalie Zaman

October 20

Thursday

3rd ♊

☽ v/c 7:17 am

☽ → ♋ 11:28 am

Color of the day: Turquoise
Incense of the day: Balsam

A Spell to Remember Dreams

If you want to learn to remember your dreams better, one of the easiest ways involves only a bottle of water, a marker, and a pen and notebook. Write the word "remember" on the bottle of water with the marker. Keep this bottle of water only for your dream work. Last thing before your head hits the pillow at night, take a sip of the water. First thing in the morning, before you are completely awake, take another sip of the water, then immediately start recording what you remember from your dreams in the notebook. With practice, you will find that you recall more and more from your dreams. Your dreams speak an intimate and personal language just for you, and over time you start to learn and understand what they are trying to teach you.

Charlie Rainbow Wolf

October 21

Friday

3rd ♋

Color of the day: Rose
Incense of the day: Yarrow

An Autumn Spell for Banishing and Balancing

As the leaves change color and fall around us, we are reminded that pieces of ourselves that no longer serve us must die. So what'll it be? Perhaps a wallowing sense of sadness that's a residual from childhood? Maybe a streak of anger that you can't seem to break? A bad habit or constant pessimism?

In addition to exploring emotionally therapeutic routes, such as art, counseling, healthy diet, and exercise, you can create a bit of magick to help usher out these forces during the glory of the dying season.

Simply gather a handful of fallen leaves and write negative things on them that summarize these sensations. These can be pictures, symbols, words, or short sentences—get creative! One by one, carefully burn these dead leaves with the flame of a black candle while declaring:

I release you now, this autumntide.
So mote it be.

Raven Digitalis

October 22

Saturday

3rd ♋

☽ v/c 3:14 pm

4th Quarter 3:14 pm

☽ → ♌ 3:34 pm

☉ → ♏ 7:46 pm

Color of the day: Indigo
Incense of the day: Patchouli

Spell of the Spider Woman (to Balance Libra and Scorpio Energies)

Two of the most different signs in the zodiac lie right next to each other: Libra and Scorpio. Some astrology historians say there used to be a thirteenth sign—the Spider Woman—in between Libra and Scorpio. Libra, ruled by Venus, is associated with balance, sociability, and a love of beauty, romance, and relationships. Scorpio, ruled by Mars and Pluto, is associated with intensity, focus, solitude, loyalty, sexuality, and force of will. The Spider Woman bridges these divergent qualities.

Find an image of a woman and one of a spider, and place them on your altar; they may be realistic or magical. Each day for a week, move these images closer together until they are lying on top of each another, and think about bridging these opposing qualities in your own life. Can your intensity be balanced with a love of beauty for a more lighthearted energy? Can your fierce loyalty be balanced with sociability?

Peg Aloi

NOTES:

October 23

Sunday

4th ♌

Color of the day: Yellow
Incense of the day: Marigold

Sukkot ends

Be Brave

Every autumn, I grieve the end of swimming season. October 23 is the latest I have ever swum in Lake Ontario. To truly swim, one's crown chakra must fully submerge. Brrr.

Each of us has our own ways of challenging and strengthening ourselves—marathons, polar dips, elaborate tasks. In his *Language of Mastery* series, Robert Tennyson Stevens teaches how to "use" fear as motivation toward faith and courage. We can transform fear. Today, be brave. Meditate.

Sit in a safe place. Breathe deeply and sink into a meditative state. Look at what you fear: poverty, illness, violence, threats, your history, etc. Feel fear grip you. Now lengthen your breath, and transform the energy. Say:

> With this energy, I feed my fire, growing strong and courageous. Where once was fear, now lives faith. I felt afraid, but found my courage. Fear transformed into faith and courage. I am brave.
>
> Dallas Jennifer Cobb

 October 24

Monday

4th ♌

☽ v/c 8:21 am
☽ → ♍ 11:16 pm

Color of the day: White
Incense of the day: Lily

Wisdom and Serenity Spell

Samhain and Halloween are just around the corner! Witches are in vogue at this time of year, and everybody wants to pepper you with questions and/or spell requests, or to have you check out their haunted house. Seems to me that this is a perfect time to cast a spell for the patience and the wisdom to answer questions with poise and integrity and to the best of your ability. After all, you are setting an example when you answer questions about the Craft—so stand up and set an outstanding one! Say these words:

> Samhain is just around the corner now,
>
> Help me answer the questions of why and how?
>
> Grant me serenity and wisdom that lasts,
>
> As I am an ambassador for my Craft.
>
> Ellen Dugan

October 25

Tuesday

4ħ ♏

Color of the day: Red
Incense of the day: Ylang-ylang

house Sealing

Sealing your home is a great way to prevent negative energies, bad vibes, and even roaming spirits from gaining entry and nestling in. After giving your house a good physical cleaning, mix together some spring water and sea salt. Using a rosemary sprig, sprinkle the saltwater around the house, moving counterclockwise through the rooms and lighting a white candle in each room. To seal the house, take a small dish of olive oil and saltwater from room to room, placing a dot at all four corners of every window and door. Using the saltwater, draw a pentagram in the middle of each window and door. Then state:

> I seal this window/door from any
> energies or entities not in tune with
> my higher power. This window/door
> is sealed.

Proceed from room to room until you've completed every entry. Let the candles burn down safely, and pour any leftover saltwater across the threshold of your front door.

Mickie Mueller

October 26

Wednesday

4ħ ♏

☽ v/c 2:33 pm

Color of the day: Topaz
Incense of the day: Bay laurel

Mourning Braid Spell

In our American culture, we seem to have forgotten that it's okay to mourn our losses. Rarely do we see anyone in black as a symbol of mourning, nor do we often see black armbands or other symbols of great loss in someone's life.

If we Pagans wish to mark such a loss, one idea is to make a mourning braid, either in your own hair or out of black cording or fabric. If you choose to do the braid in your hair, you may want to consult a professional for assistance in dyeing a lock of it black without staining your skin or clothing.

For a cloth braid, if possible, cut a few strips from a black garment that once belonged to your loved one, or you can purchase and use black cloth or cording.

As you braid the pieces together, think about your loss. There is often a threefold path involved. Say whatever you need to, and if you cry, put the tears into the braid. Wear the braid under or over your clothes for as long as you feel is necessary, and be blessed.

Thuri Calafia

October 27
Thursday

4th ♏

☽ → ♎ 9:51 am

Color of the day: Crimson
Incense of the day: Jasmine

Fossil Magick

Fossils carry unique and powerful energies. They come from deep within the earth and help to anchor us there. If you have difficulty grounding, you can carry a fossil with you or place one on your altar. During ritual, the fossil can keep you from becoming disconnected by giving you a focal point. If you're at a public ritual, keep the fossil in your pocket and touch it often to keep you grounded. Ammonite fossils form in a spiral pattern, which is a goddess symbol and a symbol of life. Also, jet and petrified wood are good choices to help ground and balance you.

Charlynn Walls

 October 28
Friday

4th ♎

Color of the day: Coral
Incense of the day: Vanilla

Break a Curse Spell

This spell will help break a curse and send it back, even if you don't know the source. You'll need three candles: one red, one white, and one black. You'll also need a stick or twig that you found on the ground. (Don't break one off a tree.)

Bless the candles and light each one. Before the candles, lay the twig. Concentrate on the curse or problem. Don't think about the person who may have cursed you—this isn't a spell of revenge. When you feel you've raised enough energy and the time is right, extinguish each candle. Then break the twig in two. In a strong voice, say:

Spirits red, spirits white, spirits black,

Break this curse and send it back!

Throw the twig outside, and don't use these candles for any other spells.

James Kambos

October 29

Saturday

4th ♎

☽ v/c 6:09 am

☽ → ♏ 10:01 pm

Color of the day: Brown
Incense of the day: Rue

Blessing a Conical hat

Though stereotypical, the conical hat has become symbolic of the power and image of Witches. This hat, once a popular style, has been revived by some modern Witches as an emblem of pride. The brim is said to denote the magic circle, while the point symbolizes the cone of power—energy generated by Witches in ritual. A consecrated hat can be a source of protection and magic in the guise of a costume accessory.

To begin, obtain a suitable hat made of some type of fabric (as opposed to plastic) and set it on your altar. Place your hands on either side of the hat, sending white light from your hands into it while saying:

Circle of magic, cone of power,

Rising to a spiritual point;

Protection and blessing I hereby shower,

With magical purpose I do anoint.

Brimming with energy, the force does surge,

My Witch's hat is hereby charged.

Michael Furie

October 30

Sunday

4th ♏

New Moon 1:38 pm

Color of the day: Amber
Incense of the day: Hyacinth

Banish Icky Stuff

The new moon is an ideal time to banish negative energies, people, and situations from your life. With Samhain just around the corner, this is the perfect opportunity to start the year fresh.

Make an anointing oil using a carrier oil such as almond oil. Add to it the following oils:

 2 drops black pepper oil

 2 drops cypress oil

 2 drops grapefruit oil

 2 drops lime oil

 2 drops rosemary oil

 2 drops vetivert oil

 2 drops yarrow oil (or a pinch of dried)

Shake the bottle of oil well to mix it thoroughly. Stand outside under the new moon, and anoint yourself with the oil. Gently rub it across your forehead, the pulse points on your neck and wrists, and your heart. Concentrate on pure white light washing through your body and cleansing you emotionally, mentally, physically, and spiritually. Chant:

> Wash over me, inside and out.
>
> Cleanse me, inside and out.
>
> Purify me, inside and out.
>
> Renew me, inside and out.
>
> Kerri Connor

NOTES:

October 31
Monday

1st ♏

☽ v/c 10:44 pm

Color of the day: Lavender
Incense of the day: Neroli

Samhain – halloween

Stare into the Darkness

It's Samhain, so the veil between the worlds is thin. Plus, the moon is in Scorpio, so it's the ideal time to gaze into your own depths, to mine for fears, and to unlock the power that they contain.

When you're alone, after dark, light a black candle. Gaze into the flame as you relax your body and let your eyes go out of focus. Allow any deep-seated fears to come to the surface, letting yourself feel them and embrace them as fully as possible. Really conjure up the feeling of wanting to feel the fear. Send your fears into the flame to be transmuted and transformed into power, excitement, and energy. Visualize a flame around yourself as you continue to burn away any stagnant or disempowered energy surrounding your fears. Blow out the candle. Feel powerful, grounded, and safe as you let the darkness permeate your inner and outer being.

Tess Whitehurst

November

At November's commencement, the veil between the worlds is thin, and spirits linger close to the realm of the living. The Mayan Day of the Dead celebration continues until the seventh day of the month, when deceased loved ones and other spirits are bid farewell with a banquet. As the month progresses, the days get shorter and colder, and we take refuge in home, family, cozy blankets and clothes, candles, and the hearth. It's a time to rest after the hard work of the year's literal or metaphorical harvest, and to honor and enjoy the fruits of our labor. Midmonth, the Leonid meteor shower makes an appearance. Named after the constellation of Leo, from which they appear to emanate, the Leonid meteors herald the smoldering end of the sun's stay in Scorpio as well as its forthcoming fiery visit to Sagittarius. While the flashiness of the shower varies, it always adds a burst of brightness to the spirit while promoting authenticity, blunt honesty, and sociability. This month, be kind to your immune system by aligning with the rhythm of the season: be sure to stay warm, stay positive, get plenty of rest, and keep your environment ordered, attractive, and bright.

Tess Whitehurst

November 1

Tuesday

1st ♏

☽ → ♐ 10:43 am

Color of the day: Scarlet
Incense of the day: Geranium

All Saints' Day

Reflection on Your Future Past

Today, focus on what people will remember after you have gone on to the Summerland.

Find a comfortable position, and dab some diluted lavender oil on your third eye. Breathe deeply and enter into a meditative state. Look ahead into your future. First impressions are important. Don't force thoughts; let them come to you. Your friends and family are gathered together. People may be missing, but you can't distinguish who. The future changes; nothing is set in stone. How are people reacting? Heavily mourning? Celebrating your life? Are they upset or at peace? Is there unfinished business? What are they saying? Is this how you want to be remembered? Can you change it if you want to? If you don't have a will, get one, and include funeral arrangements. Prepare for your future both legally and emotionally by asking the simple question "How do I want to be remembered?"

Kerri Connor

November 2

Wednesday

1st ♐

Color of the day: Yellow
Incense of the day: Marjoram

Devotional Writing Spell for a Matron Goddess

Whether you've yet to discover your matron goddess, have a new matron calling you, or have known your matron goddess(es) for a while, this spell will help you to express your devotion to her (or them).

Carve an appropriately (to you) colored pillar candle with symbols or runes that remind you of your matron (or a matron you wish to connect with). Anoint the candle and light it.

Open yourself to your matron goddess's energies. Feel the connection between the two of you as the energy grows. Ask her how she would most like you to express your love for her. She may ask for a sculpture, a season (or longer!) of service, a day of meditation, something you cook for yourself or others, or something else entirely. Leave an offering to her. Be open to her guidance, and then express that devotional energy as often as possible to build and enhance your connection to her. Be blessed.

Thuri Calafia

November 3

Thursday

1st ♐

☽ v/c 6:35 am

☽ → ♑ 11:05 pm

Color of the day: Turquoise
Incense of the day: Apricot

Saint Winefride

Saint Winefride of Wales, whose feast day is today, was a beautiful young woman who was beheaded in the 600s by a local chief named Caradoc when she attempted to flee from his unwanted advances. Not only was her head reattached by Saint Benno, effectively bringing her back to life, but also, at the spot where her head stopped rolling, a healing well appeared. According to Judika Illes in the *Encyclopedia of Mystics, Saints & Sages*, it's possible that the spring and its healing powers were known before Winefride lived, and "her legend may cloak a pre-Christian spirit or derive from Celtic traditions."

Today, invoke the powers of Saint Winefride's Holy Well by adding a tablespoon of sea salt to a bath, lighting a white candle, and invoking her name. Request support with healing any physical ailment and/or any type of sexual abuse. Soak thoroughly.

Tess Whitehurst

November 4

Friday

1st ♑

Color of the day: White
Incense of the day: Alder

Lord of Death

As we spiral down into the dark, let us celebrate the Lord of Death. Look into your personal darkness, identifying that which no longer serves you. Make lists on loose paper. Ask yourself:

What habits, routines, people, or practices do I need to let go of?
What no longer serves me?

Burn these papers in a pot or on your barbeque. As the papers flame and burn, say:

Lord of Death, take these bits, time for death and destruction.

In their place, from where they've gone, I choose resurrection.

I give you everything that doesn't make me happy, and turn my attention to the things that do.

Horned God, work your magic.

Now make lists of the people, places, habits, or practices that make you happy. Post these where you'll see them regularly.

Dallas Jennifer Cobb

November 5
Saturday

1st ♑

Color of the day: Blue
Incense of the day: Pine

Candle Magick for Spiritual Growth

Stagnation is a common occurrence, but it is something that can be overcome. The energies of the waxing moon today will promote growth and change. Choose a purple or silver candle to focus on. Visualize yourself doing the things that will bring you spiritual fulfillment. Hold the candle as you are doing your visualization, as this will help imbue your candle with your hopes and dreams.

After you have charged your candle with your intention, you may light it. This will release the positive influences that have been imbued into the candle in order to effect the change you want in your life. Let the candle burn down completely. Take the initiative and really work toward your goal of spiritual growth.

Charlynn Walls

 November 6
Sunday

1st ♑

☽ v/c 4:56 am

☽ → ♒ 8:55 am

Color of the day: Orange
Incense of the day: Hyacinth

Daylight Saving Time ends at 2:00 am

A Spell to Change the Course of Events

Today marks the end of daylight saving time, and it's a fabulous opportunity for a do-over. Think about something in your life that you would have liked to have done differently. In the last hour before the clocks change, reenact that event as best you can. At 2:00 am, you are given a rare gift to make profound changes. Pause and reflect on what was; it is going to cease to be. Set the clock back to 1:00 am to mark the end of daylight saving time, and then act out this event how you would have preferred that it came to pass. Make sure you are not imposing your will on anyone else. This is for your benefit and yours alone. This is the reality now, for the previous event was eaten in the lost hour, and it doesn't exist anymore.

Charlie Rainbow Wolf

November 7
Monday

1st ♒

2nd Quarter 2:51 pm

Color of the day: Gray
Incense of the day: Clary sage

Apple healing Spell

It's said that an apple a day keeps the doctor away. Did you know that the apple has magical healing powers? Here's an apple spell to boost your health.

Choose a lovely apple, maybe even a locally grown organic one, and make sure you clean it well. Find a relaxing, quiet place to sit, and meditate while visualizing yourself in a perfect state of health, doing all the things you like to do, feeling no pain, feeling no illness. Hold the apple in your hands, and visualize energy of strength and wellness streaming into the apple. Feel the apple pulse with energy, life, and the power of healing. Whisper into the apple:

Share with me your healing power,
by seed, sprout, tree, fruit, and flower.

Now eat the apple, and as you do so, feel it becoming one with your own cells, filling you with strength and healing energy.

Mickie Mueller

November 8
Tuesday

2nd ♒

☽ v/c 8:54 am

☽ → ♓ 4:45 pm

Color of the day: Black
Incense of the day: Basil

Election Day (general)

A Fireside Spell

In Colonial America, fire-gazing was used as a form of fire magic. It became a type of entertainment on cold evenings. This spell can be used to bring a wish into your life. Here are the items you'll need:

- A few pine cones
- 12 twigs from trees such as oak, ash, hazel, or maple
- A piece of red yarn

Lay the pine cones in the fireplace, and tie the bundle of twigs together with the yarn. As you tie them, visualize your wish being drawn to you; bind them tightly. Ignite the pine cones, and lay the twigs upon the flames. Whisper your wish, then say:

I work this spell with flame and fire,

To bring me my heart's desire.

Be it love, happiness, or good health,

Abundance, money, or wealth.

Sacred flames, hear what I say,

Bring my wish, and let me have my way.
James Kambos

NOTES:

November 9
Wednesday

2nd ♓

Color of the day: White
Incense of the day: Honeysuckle

Crystals of Protection

To protect your home and property, gather a number of quartz crystals (as many as there are rooms in your home), a large bowl to set them in, and some frankincense and a censer. Light the frankincense in the censer, and as the smoke drifts into the air, hold each of the crystals in the smoke to cleanse it and give it purpose. Once all the crystals have been censed and placed together in the bowl, hold your hands over the bowl and say:

> Crystals of the sacred land,
> join together to guard this home;
> harm and danger are now banned
> by web of light in every room.

Place one crystal in each room so that the guardians are fully distributed for thorough protection.

Michael Furie

November 10
Thursday

2nd ♓

☽ v/c 6:16 pm

☽ → ♈ 8:45 pm

Color of the day: Crimson
Incense of the day: Nutmeg

Cookie Monster Magic

Sesame Street debuted on PBS today in 1969. Lovable characters such as the manic, blue Cookie Monster, whose simple—and often correct—philosophy that more cookies equals more happiness, can teach us much about spellcasting. His rhythmically stated intention, repeated three times, never fails to yield positive results. Use his method to bring abundance into your life by way of cookies (because everyone knows that cookies make everything better).

Bake a batch of your favorite cookies, and infuse them with your desire à la *Sesame Street* as you prepare them:

A is for ABUNDANCE, it's good enough for me!

B is for BONANZA, it's like abundance but times three!

C is for CORNUCOPIA, a big word that means "plenty"!

It is as I say, so mote it be!

Eat a cookie to take the magic into yourself, and watch good things happen. Share your cookies and prepare for monstrous abundance!

Natalie Zaman

NOTES:

November 11

Friday

2nd ♈

Color of the day: Pink
Incense of the day: Violet

Veterans Day

Soldiers' Blessing

On Veterans Day, we honor the people who have chosen to serve in the military. We may or may not always agree with the jobs our soldiers are sent to do, but we should always be grateful to those who are willing to serve in the armed forces. To show your appreciation for the dedication and sacrifices made by our troops, make an offering of incense and speak the following blessing:

*On this day I honor our soldiers,
both those currently on duty and our
veterans. I give thanks to those who
have served and kept our country safe
and secure. Your work is appreciated.
May soldiers currently overseas do
honorable work in the world and come
home safely. May their commanders
be wise and their intelligence true. Let
our soldiers come home to peace and
prosperity. Blessed be our soldiers.*

Emily Carlin

November 12

Saturday

2nd ♈

☽ v/c 7:45 am
☽ → ♉ 9:24 pm

Color of the day: Black
Incense of the day: Rue

Farewell, My Green Garden

Alas! The green earth has shifted for many of us in the Northern Hemisphere. To keep the memory alive, go outside to your garden (or a public community garden) and offer some crystals to the cold earth. Bring to mind images of vibrant growth and lush vegetables, fruits, and flowers. Imagine the glory of the warm season by visualizing the sun's essence lying dormant beneath the soil.

Offer your little crystals by planting them in and around the garden bed. To give the garden an early energetic boost for next year, lean toward the ground and whisper into the earth:

*I can feel the heartbeat of the earth; the
sun now gestates for spring. Gather
in strength and fortitude; rise swiftly,
please, this coming year!*

Raven Digitalis

November 13

Sunday

2nd ♉

Color of the day: Yellow
Incense of the day: Marigold

Spell for Increasing Prosperity

This spell acknowledges habits that can sabotage our prosperity, such as spending money frivolously. On your altar, place some nuts or beans, a dollar bill, and a green candle. Place the nuts or beans on top of the dollar bill; these are a reminder that you can draw upon your resources to meet your needs without spending money. Light the green candle each day and think of how you can avoid spending money that day. Can you make dinner at home instead of getting take-out? Can you fix that hole in your jeans instead of buying a new pair? Can you read a book instead of paying to stream video? Each day you light the candle, try to count your blessings and be aware of how little you need to survive and be happy. The beans or nuts represent the bounty of your life: health, friends, family, work. All of these are more important than money.

Peg Aloi

 November 14

Monday

2nd ♉

☽ v/c 8:52 am

Full Moon 8:52 am

☽ → ♊ 8:23 pm

Color of the day: Ivory
Incense of the day: Narcissus

Full Frost Moon

November is a transitional time of the year, as it becomes less autumnal and more winter-like every day. Welcome the spirit of Papa Frost or Old Jack Frost in his many guises into your magick, and put the freeze on a problematic situation.

Tonight, the full moon rises on a Monday, so we have a double dose of lunar energy at play. As the moon rises, write down the problem you are facing on a slip of paper. Then tuck it inside a paper cup, fill the cup with water, and, if it is cold enough outdoors, place the cup outside and let it freeze overnight. If not, place the water-filled cup in the freezer. Then repeat this spell:

On this enchanted night of the November Frost Moon,

May Lady Luna hear my call and grant me a boon.

The leaves are falling down, the weather is turning cold,

So I'll use ice magick to put this problem on hold.

Old Jack Frost, now put the freeze on this problem for me,

Bringing harm to none, and as I will, so mote it be.

Ellen Dugan

NOTES:

November 15
Tuesday

3rd ♊

Color of the day: Maroon
Incense of the day: Bayberry

Shadow Dance Spell

As the moon is just past full today, it is the perfect time to begin shadow work that can continue on until the dark moon to be grounded. Choose a shadow energy you most wish to work with for this cycle. In an extra-protective circle, inscribe a black candle with all the qualities of the shadow you're working with. Anoint the candle and address it thusly:

> You represent the _____ shadow side of me, and your ways are a mystery. I hold the light, however (light the candle), so I can dance us into balance. As this candle burns, so may the light in me overcome any power this shadow holds over me. So mote it be.

If you are able and choose to do so, dance around your altar (or simply do so in your mind), imagining the form of this shadow dancing with you. Remember that our shadows are always with us, but by dancing with them, we can keep them in sight and, therefore, at bay. Let your shadow know this truth at every turn. Be blessed.

Thuri Calafia

November 16

Wednesday

3rd ♊

☽ v/c 5:58 am

☽ → ♋ 7:57 pm

Color of the day: Topaz
Incense of the day: Lilac

Wisdom of the Circumstances

Many people, by Wednesday, midweek, are dealing with some stressful and frustrating situations that have developed and whose circumstances they'd like to help change. Wednesday has both Mercurial associations and connections to the Norse god Odin. Odin is credited with being gifted the knowledge of the runes while he was hanging voluntarily from a branch of Yggdrasil (the World Tree). Let us call upon Odin's wisdom and Mercury's sharpened energy for communication and focus! Draw three runes as a simple divination to ask for advice on how you might change the circumstances of a situation currently causing you frustration. If you have a set of runes, use those. If you do not, simply draw the runes on slips of paper and pull them from a bowl or container. You can journal about the results and your interpretations; you may gain more insight into their meaning as the day goes on.

Blake Octavian Blair

 November 17

Thursday

3rd ♋

Color of the day: White
Incense of the day: Carnation

Rise above Procrastination

I've been putting off writing this spell…oh, let's face it: we all procrastinate from time to time. Some people thrive on that last-minute burst of adrenaline to cross the finish line, but if you find that your procrastination leaves you stressed to the limit, here's a spell to help you overcome it.

You'll need a 3 x 6-inch piece of paper and a seven-day jar candle. On the paper, draw two eyes. Draw in the pupil on the right eye, but leave the pupil on the left eye totally blank. Below the two eyes, write the goal, project, or whatever you need to accomplish. Use a glue stick to attach the paper to the candle. Put the candle on your desk or wherever you'll see it giving you the one-eyed stare. Every time you work on your goal, light the candle. When you complete your goal, you can draw in the other pupil and celebrate!

Mickie Mueller

November 18
Friday

3rd ♋

☽ v/c 5:02 pm

☽ → ♌ 10:14 pm

Color of the day: Purple
Incense of the day: Cypress

Spell for Protection from Nightmares

Stress can produce unpleasant dreams and disrupt sleep. Lavender is calming and can help prolong sleep and ease the stressful thoughts that can lead to nightmares. Place a bowl of saltwater beneath your bed, and before you go to bed, place a few drops of lavender on the surface of the water (do this each night until dreams improve). In addition, before sleeping, think back over the day's events in reverse order. This can help diffuse mental stress, which can sometimes cause nightmares to occur as the brain attempts to problem-solve during sleep. You may not find immediate answers or solutions, but sometimes insights may arrive in dreams. Try not to obsess over anything; briefly acknowledge situations and tell yourself you will "sleep on it." Breathe deeply, and briefly tense and release each set of muscles, from head to toe. Add more lavender so you can smell the relaxing scent.

Peg Aloi

November 19
Saturday

3rd ♌

Color of the day: Brown
Incense of the day: Patchouli

Release Grief Spell

In November, nature transitions into winter. This is a good time to work magic to free ourselves from feelings of grief. On a piece of paper, using blue ink, write down the source(s) of your grief. It could be death or divorce; whatever the cause, write it down. Then cut or tear the paper into tiny pieces and place in a dark-colored bowl. Sprinkle the pieces of paper generously with salt. Next, pour about a cup of water into the bowl and stir counterclockwise. Let this mixture sit overnight. The next day, take the bowl outside and pour the contents around a weed. Walk away. As the saltwater kills the weed and as nature moves closer to winter, your feelings of grief will begin to fade.

James Kambos

November 20

Sunday

3rd ♌

Color of the day: Amber
Incense of the day: Frankincense

Banish the Winter Blues

During the later months of the year, the days get shorter and the nights become longer. To bring a little light back into your life, brighten the colors of your altar by adding some yellow to represent the sun today. Spruce up the altar with some fresh flowers and candles from the florist as well. Add anything that is bright and vibrant. Good color choices to complement the day of the sun include yellow, gold, and white. Placing some sunstone on the altar will also catch and reflect any candle-light, creating a lovely glow that will help banish the tedium of the winter blues.

Charlynn Walls

 November 21

Monday

3rd ♌
☽ v/c 3:33 am
4th Quarter 3:33 am
☽ → ♍ 4:34 am
☉ → ♐ 4:22 pm

Color of the day: White
Incense of the day: Lily

Tarot Spell for Safety During Travel

Since this time of year often brings travel, it's a good idea to consider safety. For this spell, you'll need the tarot cards the Knight of Wands, the World, and Strength, as well as a red, a white, and a black candle. Place the black candle to the left, the white candle to the right, and the red candle in the middle of your working table or altar. In front of the red candle, set the tarot cards in a semicircle shape, with the Knight of Wands on the left, the World in the middle, and Strength on the right. Light the black candle and then the white candle to create a flow of energy. Visualize your trip and light the red candle, saying:

Protected from harm, trouble avoided,

Strength and security the whole way through.

Start on the journey, successful voyage,

Power of magic, protection imbue.

Hold the visualization for as long as you can, then extinguish the candles.

Michael Furie

NOTES:

 November 22

Tuesday

4th ♏

☽ v/c 12:41 pm

Color of the day: Red
Incense of the day: Ginger

A Spell of Thanksgiving

This is the time of year when many people's thoughts are turning toward what they are thankful to have in their lives. A very easy spell of appreciation is to recite the following:

Before me, thankful,

Behind me, thankful,

Above me, thankful,

Below me, thankful,

Around me, thankful,

Within me, thankful.

For the bounty in my life, I am thankful.

*For the challenges in my life,
I am thankful.*

May I walk my days in gratitude.

For this, I am thankful.

Charlie Rainbow Wolf

November 23
Wednesday

4th ♏

☽ → ♎ 2:42 pm

Color of the day: White
Incense of the day: Lavender

To See Clearly Through Anger

We all have times when our emotions overcome our good judgment. Anger, in particular, has the ability to distort our perception and understanding. If you suspect that your anger is clouding your thoughts, take time out for a few deep breaths. When you are calm, recite the following:

Let my anger depart and soothe my wounded heart.

Remove the scales from upon my eyes, help me to see through hate and lies.

No more my thoughts shall clouded be, instead it shall be the truth I see.

Let me understand with clarity and return to a mind of acuity.

Repeat as necessary while the problem persists.

— Emily Carlin

November 24
Thursday

4th ♎

Color of the day: Purple
Incense of the day: Myrrh

Thanksgiving Day

Throwing the Turkey Bones

Throwing the bones is a traditional Hoodoo means of divination. Chicken bones are most commonly used, but on Thanksgiving Day, think big and work with what's at hand. After your Thanksgiving feast, clean and dry (and paint if you wish) four bones from your turkey: a leg bone, one of the small single bones from one of the wings, the wishbone, and a broken bone of your choice.

Blindfold your querent, and mix and arrange the bones on a table in front of the person. Make predictions based on what he or she selects:

- Choose the large leg bone, and big change is afoot.

- Choose the small bone, and expect small changes in day-to-day life.

- Choose the wishbone—your wish is granted!

- Choose the broken bone, and know that something needs to come to an end—perhaps a bad habit or a project that needs finishing.

Natalie Zaman

NOTES:

 November 25

Friday

4♄ ♎

☽ v/c 8:52 am

Color of the day: Rose
Incense of the day: Mint

Saint Catherine

Saint Catherine of Alexandria—who is aligned with such magical superstars as Athena, Fortuna, and Hypatia—is honored on this day. Although she's no longer recognized as an official saint, her spiritual vibration is palpable and potent, and she can be petitioned effectively for help with romantic matters, especially related to marriage and lifelong partners. To do this, place an image of Saint Catherine on your altar. Add a few drops of essential oil of sandalwood to some sunflower oil, and anoint a red pillar candle with the oil. Place the candle on a holder, and sprinkle a pinch of gold glitter on and around it. Earnestly request that Saint Catherine powerfully intervene to help bring about ideal conditions in your love life. (You can hold a specific desire in mind, but it's best to trust the details and outcome to her.) Then thank her. Light the candle and allow it to burn all the way down, extinguishing and lighting again as necessary.

Tess Whitehurst

November 26

Saturday

4th ♎

☽ → ♏ 3:01 am

Color of the day: Gray
Incense of the day: Sandalwood

Spell for the hearth and home

The winter holiday season is upon us. Why not celebrate with a hearth and home spell? No matter where you live, the hearth is often the heart of the home. These days, that "hearth" is often the kitchen. Call on Hestia, the Greek goddess of the hearth flame. Hestia was a powerful deity, as she was traditionally the first and last of the gods to be invoked.

To begin, light a red candle and display it safely in a place of honor. Then say:

Hestia, goddess of the hearth's flame,

I honor your power now and call your name.

Watch over our home and bless us all during the holidays,

May your power shine forth and brighten up these dark winter days.

Let the candle burn out in a safe place. If you wish, you can rework this spell throughout the holiday season.

Ellen Dugan

November 27

Sunday

4th ♏

☽ v/c 4:48 pm

Color of the day: Gold
Incense of the day: Heliotrope

A Candle Spell: Your Voice in the Universe

If you feel that your own personal voice in life has gone unheard lately, try this spell to increase your presence and shift your energy from an introspective place into one that is more extroverted—at least temporarily. You can repeat this exercise whenever it feels like social pressures are too overwhelming, or during times when you are required to be socially active but feel like isolating yourself.

Begin by making "big" body movements. By making yourself big, and by using vocal intonation, your field of energy expands. Jump up and down, windmill your arms, flail around, and dance like no one is watching (please note that no one should be watching!). Vocally make your presence known to the universe by declaring:

Me! Free! Me! Free! Me! Free!

After you've sufficiently stirred up your energy, close your eyes and place your hands on your Vishuddha (throat) chakra. Visualize the energy that you've just raised as a vibrant blue color that surrounds your body.

Consciously direct and channel all of this energy into your throat. See your throat as expansive and expressive—just like you were moments earlier. When you feel you've recharged this area with the blue light of communication, regularly practice speaking your mind with eloquence and grace.

Raven Digitalis

NOTES:

November 28
Monday

4th ♏

☽ → ♐ 3:46 pm

Color of the day: Gray
Incense of the day: Rosemary

Prosperity Spell for a Cause

Today is Cyber Monday, a day when millions of people flock online to purchase holiday gifts. However, as the old adage goes, it is better to give than to receive. Additionally, we know that what we put out into the universe influences what we get in return. Therefore, to attract greater prosperity, it is good magick to share what prosperity we already have with others in need.

Today, pick an organization or charity that does good in the world by supporting and effecting beneficial change for social justice, environmental or conservation issues, or another cause dear to you. Then make a donation online, even if it is for only a few dollars—every bit counts! This is a magickal act of reciprocity: by sharing our treasure, we open ourselves up for the universe to bring us even more!

Blake Octavian Blair

November 29

Tuesday

4th ♐
New Moon 7:18 am
Color of the day: White
Incense of the day: Cinnamon

Spiritual Resurrection

Ancient legends from Romania claim that each year, on this night, vampires rise from their graves after a year-long sleep to search for human blood. Taken metaphorically, this is the time for spiritual resurrection, to awaken your spirit in areas where it may have been sleeping, and choose to renew, revitalize, and drink in new life.

Use the new moon to work a resurrection spell. On a white sheet of paper, write three of your desires that may have been "sleeping." Place the paper face down in front of you. Light a white candle and say:

With clarity, intention, and conscious will, I call in spirit to inspire me.

Turn over your list of desires and say:

With candle and new-moon light, I resurrect these desires.

Hold the paper in both hands and exhale on it. Say:

Blessed with the breath of life, may you find new life tonight and grow with the waxing moon.

Dallas Jennifer Cobb

November 30

Wednesday

1st ♐
☽ v/c 11:08 pm
Color of the day: Brown
Incense of the day: Honeysuckle

Renew Your Spirit

Whether things are going well in your life or not, it never hurts to renew your spirit and give yourself a fresh start. Use this meditative ritual bath to cleanse and renew your spirit.

Draw a warm bath and add the following herbs or oils to the water: basil, black pepper, chamomile, cinnamon, cypress, juniper, lemon, myrrh, and pine. If you're using oils, use only a couple of drops of each. Submerge yourself in the bath as far as you can. Visualize white light cleansing you and your spirit. Feel it in and around you, cleansing and leaving everything in its path shiny, bright, and new. You and your spirit are glowing and refreshed.

Soak for at least fifteen minutes and then drain the tub, allowing any negative energy to flow down the drain as it leaves you through the water. As you step out of the tub, thank your deities for their support.

Kerri Connor

December

December, in the minds of many, is both the quintessential winter month and one of the busiest months of the year. It is a month full of joyous celebrations from many traditions. Advent, Bodhi Day, Saturnalia, Kwanzaa, Pancha Ganapati, Christmas, Hanukkah, and Yule are just a small selection of festivals that have their calendrical home in the month of December.

The themes of light (literal, energetic, and metaphorical), wisdom, and goodwill are a common thread among many of the celebrations. This is a good time of year to remember that despite our differences, we have much in common with one other. In a modern culture where many of us practice religious and spiritual pluralism to some degree, December presents more than one holy festival for each of us to nurture our spirit.

In the Northern Hemisphere, the winter solstice marks the official start of winter—a season of introspection. Though the land appears outwardly to be in a quiet slumber, we know that beneath the soil, down in the roots and in the dens of animals, there is a process of incubative growth occurring. Once again, the seasons of our soul align in harmony with the seasons of nature.

Blake Octavian Blair

December 1

Thursday

1st ♐

☽ → ♑ 3:52 am

Color of the day: White
Incense of the day: Mulberry

holiday Survival Kit Spell

Amid the hustle and bustle of the holiday season, many a Witch has nearly collapsed with exhaustion. There is so much to carry on a broomstick! To combat the holiday blues, create a holiday survival kit.

In a small bag, gather together a non-plastic bottle filled with water, plus some nuts, whole-grain crackers, and fruit (add jerky or cheese if you're an omnivore) for when you're running and there's nothing to eat fast but, well, fast food. Also include a lavender sachet for a quick calm-down after you've schlepped all those bags to the car and fallen into the driver's seat yet again. Inhale deeeeeeply…slooooooowwwly. Ahh.

Next, add a coin for flipping for quick divinations on everything from gift choices to driving directions. Add some ginger extract or tea bags for indigestion, and a small bell for calling the fairies to return your good humor.

Waft a favorite incense over the bag to charge it, commanding it to remind you it's here when you need it. Happy shopping and blessed be!

Thuri Çalafia

 December 2

Friday

1st ♑

Color of the day: Pink
Incense of the day: Vanilla

Releasing Fear

Winter is a great time for introspective magickal workings. It is a time to really assess whether our thoughts and feelings are in alignment. In order to grow as individuals, we need to release any fears that may be hindering us. In order to do this, you will want to be in a comfortably warm room so you can sit on the floor or stretch out. Have a small bowl or chalice with water in it nearby. The room should be quiet, and the lights should be dimmed. Feel your heart beat, and become aware of your own breath.

Ask yourself what you fear. Is it conducive to continuing on your spiritual path? Is it a burden to continually worry about this fear? Name your fear as you cup the bowl or chalice between your hands. Let your fear wash out of you and into the water. Continue to do this until all of your fears have been named. Once you are ready, set the cup aside, and breathe again and find your heart's rhythm. When you are settled, you can get up and pour the water down your drain. Watch as your fears go along with it.

Charlynn Walls

December 3

Saturday

1st ♑

☽ v/c 5:16 am

☽ → ♒ 2:44 pm

Color of the day: Black
Incense of the day: Magnolia

Mari

The International Day of the Basque Language (today) is a day designated to honor this most mysterious of languages, spoken by residents of the Pyrenees Mountains between France and Spain. Without any known relatives, Basque is suspected to be very ancient, perhaps the last surviving vestige of a language family that was once widespread across Europe. Mari is the beloved, earthy, cave-dwelling moon and nature goddess of the Basques. She sits atop their ancient pantheon and is an extremely positive and powerful representation of the feminine divine. To petition her help with prosperity and personal power, cleanse a white quartz point in sunlight and tie a dollar bill and a fresh flower around it with red yarn. Visit a cave or (alternatively) a hollowed-out area at the base of a tree. Connect with Mari's essence while feeling power and prosperity flow into your energy field. Then leave the crystal in the cave.

Tess Whitehurst

December 4

Sunday

1st ♒

Color of the day: Yellow
Incense of the day: Eucalyptus

A Prayer to Shango

In the Santeria pantheon, Shango is the orisha of fire, lightning, and thunder. His colors are red and white: red for passion and white for peace. Today, on Shango's day, restore your equilibrium by crafting a bracelet to carry his spirit with you. String an equal number of red and white beads on a length of jelly cord to fit your wrist. As you string the beads and tie the cord to connect them (make sure your bracelet is a never-ending circle of alternating beads), call to him:

Lord of lightning

And the calm of the storm,

Shango, bestow your blessings on me.

It is important to leave an offering for an orisha when you ask for his or her help. Thank Shango by leaving one or more of his favorite foods out on a red and white cloth: bananas, okra, or a bowl of red palm oil.

Natalie Zaman

December 5

Monday

1st ♈ ♒

☽ v/c 6:23 am

☽ → ♓ 11:31 pm

Color of the day: Silver
Incense of the day: Hyssop

Peace and Goodwill

During the winter season, a lot of holidays are celebrated that bring families together. This can be a blessing as well as a hardship. Expenses go up, nerves wear thin, and people get on each other's nerves. Keep the peace by using this spell to help everyone get along.

In the room where people gather most often, place a green bowl (glass is best) filled with as many of the following stones, herbs, and oils as possible: calcite, carnelian, celestite, chrysocolla, quartz, hematite, jasper, lepidolite, malachite, moonstone, obsidian, sodalite, tourmaline, amber, apple blossom, bayberry, cedar, coltsfoot, costmary, cypress, dragon's blood, elderberry, frankincense, gardenia, juniper, lavender, mistletoe, and myrrh.

Place all the items in the green bowl and mix well. Place your hand in the bowl and say:

Keep this family at peace.

Place the bowl in a prominent location where its magic will be able to work on all of those who come into close proximity of it.

Kerri Connor

NOTES:

December 6

Tuesday

1st ♒

Color of the day: Red
Incense of the day: Geranium

A Spell to Release Tension

At this time of year, it's easy to get caught up in hectic preparations. But in order to offer the best of yourself to your loved ones, you have to be at your very best, first.

One way to help maintain your equilibrium is to take time to relax at the end of each day. Sit in a peaceful setting, away from the family and the television. Have a cup of soothing tea, such as chamomile or lemon balm. Breathe out the anxiety, then take a sip of the tea and know that you are taking in relaxation. Focus on your breath, exhaling the tension. Repeat this until the cup of tea is gone, replacing the stress and pressure with the relaxation and peacefulness that you need to cope with this wonderful but busy holiday season.

Charlie Rainbow Wolf

 December 7

Wednesday

1st ♓
2nd Quarter 4:03 am
☽ v/c 9:05 am

Color of the day: Topaz
Incense of the day: Lilac

Travel Safety Spell

Before embarking on your trip, hold a fluorite in your hand and recite the following:

I travel this day.

Great power of the west,

*Guardian of those who, like the
primal waters,*

flow from place to place.

I will depart on time.

I will arrive on time.

My road will know no obstacles.

My journey will know no hardships.

*Let my lessons from this journey
be brief.*

I will fly like the wind,

Where I want to go.

I meet those who care, safely.

I have all I intended to bring.

Thus do I conjure.

Keep the fluorite on your person while you travel.

Emily Carlin

December 8

Thursday

2nd ♓

☽ → ♈ 5:15 am

Color of the day: Purple
Incense of the day: Clove

Thor's Spell for Protection and Courage

This day of the week is named after the Norse god Thor. Thor was called the "everyman's god," and he is wildly popular with Pagans and Witches today. Since we have a waxing-moon phase, this is a perfect time to pull a little protection and courage into your life and to be thankful for the things you have, all with the help of Thor. Say these words:

I ask for the help of Thor, the Norse god of everyman.

May your strength protect me, and abundance spread across my land.

Help me to be brave and true, come what may.

I'm thankful for your blessings through all of my days.

Ellen Dugan

December 9

Friday

2nd ♈

☽ v/c 8:06 pm

Color of the day: Coral
Incense of the day: Orchid

hanging of the Greens

Decorating our homes for the holidays was traditionally called the "hanging of the greens." But as you select your Yule/Christmas tree and holiday greenery, do you realize how magically significant the evergreens are? These noble trees are the elders of the tree kingdom. They witnessed the creation of our planet and survived the ice ages.

This spell will bring protection and good fortune to your home. Before you decorate your tree, remove three pine needles from it. Place them on a green cloth with a lock of your hair. Face the tree and say:

I thank you, tree and all greenery that has been cut,

Bring me and my home good fortune and luck.

Ancient one who has seen the centuries pass,

Our bond shall forever last.

Tie up the cloth with green thread or yarn, and bury near your threshold.

James Kambos

December 10
Saturday

2nd ♈

☽ → ♉ 7:41 am

Color of the day: Gray
Incense of the day: Ivy

Gratitude

Let today be a day to live in a state of grace, cultivating gratitude for the resources that surround and support you, the people who love and care for you, and the earth that shelters and guides us. In even the smallest act, there are a multitude of things to be thankful for.

Pause while making tea and give thanks for electricity or gas and the fuels and tools to heat water. Be grateful for clean, clear, and safe drinking water that flows out of the tap. Have gratitude for the cup you drink from, the dishes in your kitchen, the kitchen itself, and your sheltering home. As you drink the tea, feel blessed by the soothing, healing liquid that nourishes and replenishes your body. Give thanks for your wondrous body! May every cell be well. As you sip your tea, whisper *thank you*, swallow, and know gratitude. Let awareness raise you into a state of grace.

Dallas Jennifer Cobb

December 11
Sunday

2nd ♉

☽ v/c 11:04 pm

Color of the day: Orange
Incense of the day: Juniper

Copal Solar Smudge

This time of year, when the days are shorter and the darkness may be wearing on many, is the perfect time to do a bit of solar magick. Smudging is a cross-cultural practice that is performed for many reasons. Copal is a popular resin used in incenses and smudges in Central and South America, and luckily a few varieties are widely available. The sun is the planetary ruler of copal, making it a great choice for our magickal purposes today. Gather a heatproof bowl or censer filled with sand or gravel, an incense charcoal, and a bit of copal resin. Light the charcoal and verbally invoke the sun in any way that you see fit. Ask that the sun infuse, charge, and bless the resin, then sprinkle a bit onto the charcoal. While wafting the smoke, visualize it as the radiant light of the sun filling your space with warmth, energy, and vitality.

Blake Octavian Blair

December 12

Monday

2nd ♉

☽ → ♊ 7:41 am

Color of the day: Lavender
Incense of the day: Lily

The Book Speaks

So there's some big problem you need to solve, some obstacle to overcome, some evil that needs banishing. How do I know? Well, here's my secret: even as you are reading them, books contain a special magic that bridges communication between the author, Higher Spirit, and the reader. Here is a great way for you to get some advice on the best course of action to take; it's an art of divination called bibliomancy.

Locate a book—not just any book, but a book that you love and that you feel is full of truths. Close your eyes and concentrate on your situation, and as you do so, flip the pages of the book back and forth until you feel that it's right to stop. Open your eyes, and the first thing you read on the page, whatever your eyes are drawn to, will have a special message that applies to your situation.

Mickie Mueller

December 13

Tuesday

2nd ♊

Full Moon 7:06 pm

Color of the day: White
Incense of the day: Basil

Full Moon Truth Spell

This full moon has the moon in Gemini and the sun traveling through Sagittarius. These are both energetic and adaptable signs that love to gather and understand information, so this is a perfect time to cast a spell to uncover truth. This spell will be cast on the information itself, as opposed to a person withholding the truth.

To begin, burn an incense of rosemary and frankincense in a cauldron, and light a white candle. On a piece of paper, write down the name of the person you think is lying to you, along with what you think he or she is lying about. Then fold the paper in half. While holding it in your hand, charge the paper with your intent and say:

Pierce through the fog of uncertainty,
let the truth be known, so mote it be!

Light the paper in the candle's flame, and drop it in the cauldron.

Michael Furie

December 14

Wednesday

3rd ♊

☽ v/c 12:58 am

☽ → ♋ 7:09 am

Color of the day: Brown
Incense of the day: Marjoram

Spell to Plan Winter Work

Spending more time indoors in winter means we can make time for projects we don't get to during warmer weather. For this spell, hand-draw a simple calendar on a piece of paper. Use colored pens and make it pleasing to look at. Then get some colored pieces of paper or sticky notes, and write your individual projects on each one (make several for projects that will take more than one day). Keep the project notes on your altar for a night or two, charging them with intention. Place the project notes on top of the calendar dates you plan to do them; if you don't get to it that day, move it to another day. Use tacks to stick the project notes on the new days. This allows you to be flexible and work according to your own time and energy. Keep the calendar in a visible but accessible place so you can move things as needed.

Peg Aloi

 December 15

Thursday

3rd ♋

☽ v/c 4:37 pm

Color of the day: Crimson
Incense of the day: Jasmine

A Fire and Ice House Blessing

As the chilly and beautiful weather surrounds us, our energies are drawn inward. We can use this opportunity to invoke protective energies for the house and home, providing a rampart of protection during the cold season.

Because magick often operates in paradigms, gather eight tealight candles and place each candle individually in a tall jar. Starting in the north and moving in a deosil (clockwise) direction, light each candle an equal distance apart around the house to form eight points representing the Wheel of the Year.

Once all the candles are safely lit, stand in the very center of your home and visualize a soft, fiery light creating the sacred Wheel of the Year, with yourself at the center. See this energy filling you and surrounding the house in a protective three-dimensional wheel of light and life. When you feel fulfilled, keep a close eye on the candles while they naturally burn out. Feel free to incorporate any additional house-cleansing rituals throughout the activity that you wish.

Raven Digitalis

December 16

Friday

3rd ♋

☽ → ♌ 8:15 am

Color of the day: White
Incense of the day: Mint

Tea for Two (or Three or More!)

There is nothing so comforting as a spot of tea, especially when it includes scones with gobs of raspberry jam and clotted cream. Afternoon tea is a bit of a luxury—we are always busy—but it is essential to remember the importance of maintaining our relationships with others. Invite friends to tea for a ritual of reconnection.

Clear a table and bless it as sacred space. Lay out your tea service and any food and hot water as if you were setting up an altar. Incorporate elements into your meal and table setting that symbolize friendship, such as pineapples, lemons, irises, yellow roses, and ivy. When everyone sits down, hold hands to form an unbroken circle and speak a spell of friendship together:

Tea and sympathy,

Friendship and empathy,

Teatime is our time to reconnect.

Then…enjoy. Savor every moment.

Natalie Zaman

 December 17

Saturday

3rd ♌

Color of the day: Indigo
Incense of the day: Pine

Food Magic for Pets

As a means of sending blessing or healing energy to our pets, we can use a bit of kitchen magic. Since so many ingredients in our food are potentially dangerous for pets (for example, garlic and onions can lead to anemia in dogs and cats, and neither animal can eat chocolate), it's not wise to mix in extra things like herbs into their food. We can, however, project energy into the food to charge it with the desired quality. If it's moist food, a power symbol can be traced in it with a knife or fork, sending energy through it into the meal. If it's dry kibble, the symbol can be traced onto the bowl before adding the food, so that the energy is absorbed into it as it's being eaten.

Michael Furie

December 18

Sunday

3rd ♌

☽ v/c 11:55 am

☽ → ♍ 12:52 pm

Color of the day: Gold
Incense of the day: Almond

Candle Spell to Remove Obstacles

Today we are in a waning-moon phase, a perfect time to remove obstacles. Plus it is Sunday, the day for success! Let's combine these enchanting energies with a candle spell to remove any obstacles in your path.

Take a golden votive candle and carve a sun symbol on it, then place it in a votive cup. Light the candle and hold the votive cup out in front of you. Now focus on the flame burning through any impediment and opening up the way to your success. Say these words:

As I hold this golden spell candle in my hands,

I empower it to send success out across the land.

Now burn with magickal purpose both bright and true,

May the way be opened for all that I wish to do.

Allow the candle to burn out in a safe place. My best wishes for your success!

Ellen Dugan

 December 19

Monday

3rd ♍

Color of the day: Ivory
Incense of the day: Rosemary

Put the Past Behind You

With the physical year coming to an end, it's time to clear out the old and make way for the new. Sometimes we have to say goodbye to people no matter how much we may want to keep them in our lives. Perhaps they don't want to be in our lives, or their being there really isn't in our best interest. Saying goodbye to these people can be really difficult, and it might not be possible to actually tell someone goodbye because they don't want to hear it. Write a letter to the person to whom you need to say goodbye. Say whatever it is you need to in order to put this behind you. Write down exactly how you feel. When you are done, drip drops of sage oil onto the paper, and place it in a fireproof container. Light the paper on fire and let it burn, sending your goodbye out into the universe.

Kerri Connor

December 20

Tuesday

3rd ♏

☽ v/c 8:56 pm

4th Quarter 8:56 pm

☽ → ♎ 9:40 pm

Color of the day: Gray
Incense of the day: Cinnamon

Paper Dolls for Peace

Witches are not the only ones who suffer from bigotry, but we certainly have had our share. Many people are persecuted every day because of their faith, race, sexual orientation, age, socioeconomic position, and more. Here's a spell to allow feelings of fellowship to ripple out into the world in order to override bigotry.

Anoint a white or blue candle with lavender oil and light it. Hold a sheet of plain white computer paper in the horizontal position (landscape), and fold it in half from left to right three times. Each time you fold, say:

Fellowship for all humankind,

Understanding spirit, body, and mind.

If you've never made paper dolls holding hands out of paper, there are easy instructions on the Internet. Cut out the paper dolls, then hold the folded paper dolls in your hands and fill them with love as you meditate. As you unfold them, see love and fellowship rippling out.

Mickie Mueller

NOTES:

December 21
Wednesday

4♏ ♎

☉ → ♑ 5:44 am

Color of the day: White
Incense of the day: Honeysuckle

Yule – Winter Solstice

Yule Log Cake

Yule is the shortest day of the year and marks the rebirth of the sun. It is a time for friends and family to gather together and celebrate the sun's return. A special treat you can make for them is a yule log cake. These are fairly easy to concoct, and you can mix in a little magick from the kitchen as well!

Early in the morning, to welcome the sun, gather your ingredients to make a simple sponge cake. Then bake it, and once cooled, spread a layer of cream or hazelnut filling onto the cake. Roll up the sponge into a log. Once you have arranged the log on the serving plate, it's time to frost it with chocolate frosting. You can sprinkle the cake with powdered sugar to simulate snow, create marzipan mushrooms, or decorate with mint and cranberries to simulate holly. No matter how you slice it, your family will appreciate the extra effort you went through to make the day special!

Charlynn Walls

December 22
Thursday

4♏ ♎

☽ v/c 2:31 pm

Color of the day: Green
Incense of the day: Myrrh

Mercury Retrograde Redux

This Mercury-retrograde period is just in time for the holiday break. Luckily, the waning moon is in the balanced air sign of Libra, so it's a nice day to take a timeout and do what Mercury retrograde periods are best for: reexamining, reevaluating, and dotting your i's and crossing your t's. Do you have any presents that still need to be purchased or wrapped? Did you remember to send cards, gifts, and/or invitations to everyone on your list? Are you totally clear about your travel plans? Anoint a white candle with rosemary oil and light it. Say:

I now summon clarity, harmony, order, and balance.

See these energies as bright white light filling your field and extending to all the areas of your life. Then, particularly in regard to things such as communication, plans, and exchanges of any sort, take some time to make sure you've got everything covered.

Tess Whitehurst

December 23
Friday

4th ♎

☽ → ♏ 9:32 am

Color of the day: Purple
Incense of the day: Thyme

Spell for the Celtic Tree Month of Birch/Beth

The Celtic lore assigning trees to months offers guidelines for magical and inner work. Birch (Beth) begins on this date and is a time of new beginnings. Birch is protective and healing, and also is associated with new endeavors, new relationships, and fertility. You can buy birch bark from your local Pagan or herb shop (or health food store), or find a peeling of birch bark from a local tree (it should pull off easily if it is ready to shed). You can make an incense with the bark, or simply keep it on your altar to receive its inspiration. You may also make a small bundle of birch twigs (tie with red or green ribbon), and place it in a prominent place (such as near the front door) for protection.

Peg Aloi

December 24
Saturday

4th ♏

Color of the day: Brown
Incense of the day: Sage

Christmas Eve

As the Wheel Turns Spell

If you're a Pagan who doesn't also celebrate the Christian holiday, you might choose tonight to take down your tree. As you do so, gather some of the dried greens and place them in a dish. Once the whole house is cleaned and the decorations are put away, take a fireproof dish and carefully burn the last of the Yule greens. If there are a lot, you'll want to do this outside. If burning just a few, you'll still want to do this near an open door or window.

As you put each sprig on the fire, think about all that came to pass this year and that which is fading away. While doing so, I like to softly and slowly sing a single line from "Deck the Halls"—the one about how quickly the old year leaves us. You may wish to use this lyric or another one that has deep meaning for you. Once all is burned, say:

The Wheel turns. I welcome the new.

Be blessed.

Thuri Calafia

December 25

Sunday

4th ♏

☽ v/c 2:22 am

☽ → ♐ 10:19 pm

Color of the day: Amber
Incense of the day: Marigold

Christmas Day – hanukkah begins

A Christmas Wish Spell

At Yule and Christmas, we celebrate the God aspect and his birth, the Sun God and Jesus. These are celebrations focusing on joy, renewal, warmth, and abundance, as we look toward spring. Early Pagan celebrations at this time of year honored the Horned God. Remnants of this are still evident at Christmas, but now reindeer fill this role.

This spell is meant to bring abundance into your life. On your altar, place a stag or reindeer decoration. Surround it with holiday symbols of virility and abundance, such as pine, pine cones, nuts, and fruit-shaped ornaments. Light a red candle. On a piece of stationery, using a gold ink craft pen, write your wish, then seal it in an envelope. Let the candle burn a while, and hide your charm. At the summer solstice, burn your written charm in a ritual fire.

James Kambos

NOTES:

December 26
Monday

4℞ ♐

Color of the day: White
Incense of the day: Clary sage

Kwanzaa begins

World Family

K wanzaa, a celebration of family, community, and culture, begins today. Created to bring focus to the collectively held values of many African cultures, Kwanzaa celebrates, honors, and seeks to perpetuate these values in modern society. The seven values central to Kwanzaa are *Umoja* (unity), *Kujichagulia* (self-determination), *Ujima* (collective work and responsibility), *Ujamaa* (cooperative economics), *Nia* (purpose), *Kuumba* (creativity), and *Imani* (faith).

Today, tap into these values in order to recognize that we are all driven toward the same purpose—to connect with our deeper values of family, community, and culture. Take each value and make a short list. Know how you (and yours) are unique, and then extend your consciousness to the ways in which we are all the same, regardless of color, culture, faith, or location. List where we connect. Say a quiet prayer:

Sharing these deeply held values,
we are one family.

Dallas Jennifer Cobb

 ## December 27
Tuesday

4℞ ♐

☽ v/c 8:45 pm

Color of the day: Black
Incense of the day: Cedar

Solar Confidence to Outshine Anxiety

A t this time of year, the sun is far away from the earth in the Northern Hemisphere. Since we recently passed the winter solstice, not to mention the craziness of Christmastime, it's a good idea to harness the light of the sun while it slowly begins its annual waxing cycle.

Carry a sunstone in one pocket and a citrine in the other (or any other solar stones you fancy). Standing outdoors in the dim sunlight, envision the solar rays descending into your body and soul. Slowly walk six large deosil (clockwise) circles while you visualize the snow and ice melting. Think about issues in your life that cause you anxiety and insecurity. Stand at the center of the circle you've just walked, and boldly declare:

As each day passes, my confidence
grows. In the name of the sun, I love
myself and all that I am!

Raven Digitalis

December 28
Wednesday

4th ♐

☽ → ♑ 10:12 am

Color of the day: Yellow
Incense of the day: Bay laurel

Tarot Polarity Spell for Prosperity

For this prosperity spell, gather the following items:

- A cauldron
- A green candle
- Incense composed of equal parts sage and cinnamon
- The tarot cards Seven of Pentacles, Five of Pentacles, and Ace of Pentacles
- A paper and pen

Place the Seven of Pentacles in front of the cauldron, the Five of Pentacles to the left, and the Ace of Pentacles to the right. The left card represents the negative polarity (poverty), and the right card represents the extreme positive (wealth), with the middle card showing financial stability (the goal). On the paper, draw a dollar sign (the symbol of money), and set the paper on the middle card.

Light the candle and incense in the cauldron. Raise power to charge the cards and paper. To focus the intent, say:

Prosperity, now come to me;
abundance, manifest. So mote it be.

Light the paper in the candle, dropping it into the cauldron over the incense to release the spell.

Michael Furie

NOTES:

December 29

Thursday

4th ♑

New Moon 1:53 am

Color of the day: Turquoise
Incense of the day: Carnation

Moon Banishment Spell

Now and then, we all have a suspicion that somebody is being dishonest and trying to deceive us. The new moon is a great time for dealing with the unseen and also for banishment magick. Here is a spell that is perfectly designed to harness these characteristics of the new moon.

Print an image of the Moon card from the tarot. (Don't use an actual tarot card; the image will be destroyed!) On the back of the printed image, write a petition of intention to banish all unseen deception being perpetrated against you, harming none, for the highest good, and be sure to sign it. In your fireplace or a fire-safe cauldron or bowl, ritually burn the image and exclaim:

> *Power of the Moon, I ask thee, please banish all deception perpetrated against me. May it be for the highest good. Blessed be!*

> Blake Octavian Blair

 December 30

Friday

1st ♑

☽ v/c 3:07 am

☽ → ♒ 8:29 pm

Color of the day: Rose
Incense of the day: Yarrow

A Sticky Spell for Protection

For this protection spell, you'll need a pound of powdered or icing sugar, a jar with a shaker top (a Parmesan cheese–type jar is awesome), and something small that is personal to you, such as a ring or a hair tie. Put the item in the jar with the sugar. Focusing on establishing a boundary, start walking the perimeter of your property, shaking out a little bit of the sugar with every step. Make sure you'll have enough to go all the way around your property line. Once you've completed the circuit, go back in your house. Envision energy rising up out of the sugar and meeting over the center of your house, like an invisible tent. Anyone wishing you harm is going to get stuck in the sugary stickiness, while those bringing you goodness will be able to pass through freely.

> Charlie Rainbow Wolf

December 31

Saturday

1st ♒

Color of the day: Blue
Incense of the day: Rue

New Year's Eve

Guiding Change

The new year is always a time for change, although we're not always sure if that change will be for good or ill. Here's a little spell for guiding the changes in your life to be as positive as possible.

Take a moment to reflect on the year that has passed and the possible changes that will come with the new year. Then recite the following:

Change is in the air.

Things are shifting, moving, evolving.

Change is here.

Things are growing, stretching, shedding old skins.

May I grow easily.

May I learn my lessons swiftly.

May I shed that which no longer serves painlessly.

May I evolve smoothly,

Into something more,

Something higher,

Something greater.

Change serves me.

Change is my ally.

I stretch, I learn, I grow.

I am change and change is me.

I am ready.

So mote it be.

Emily Carlin

NOTES:

Daily Magical Influences

Each day is ruled by a planet that possesses specific magical influences:

Monday (Moon): peace, healing, caring, psychic awareness, purification.

Tuesday (Mars): passion, sex, courage, aggression, protection.

Wednesday (Mercury): conscious mind, study, travel, divination, wisdom.

Thursday (Jupiter): expansion, money, prosperity, generosity.

Friday (Venus): love, friendship, reconciliation, beauty.

Saturday (Saturn): longevity, exorcism, endings, homes, houses.

Sunday (Sun): healing, spirituality, success, strength, protection.

Lunar Phases

The lunar phase is important in determining best times for magic.

The waxing moon (from the new moon to the full moon) is the ideal time for magic to draw things toward you.

The full moon is the time of greatest power.

The waning moon (from the full moon to the new moon) is a time for study, meditation, and little magical work (except magic designed to banish harmful energies).

Astrological Symbols

The Sun	☉		Aries	♈
The Moon	☽		Taurus	♉
Mercury	☿		Gemini	♊
Venus	♀		Cancer	♋
Mars	♂		Leo	♌
Jupiter	♃		Virgo	♍
Saturn	♄		Libra	♎
Uranus	♅		Scorpio	♏
Neptune	♆		Sagittarius	♐
Pluto	♇		Capricorn	♑
			Aquarius	♒
			Pisces	♓

The Moon's Sign

The moon's sign is a traditional consideration for astrologers. The moon continuously moves through each sign in the zodiac, from Aries to Pisces. The moon influences the sign it inhabits, creating different energies that affect our daily lives.

Aries: Good for starting things but lacks staying power. Things occur rapidly but quickly pass. People tend to be argumentative and assertive.

Taurus: Things begun now do last, tend to increase in value, and become hard to alter. Brings out an appreciation for beauty and sensory experience.

Gemini: Things begun now are easily changed by outside influence. Time for shortcuts, communications, games, and fun.

Cancer: Stimulates emotional rapport between people. Pinpoints need, supports growth and nurturance. Tend to domestic concerns.

Leo: Draws emphasis to the self, to central ideas or institutions, away from connections with others and emotional needs. People tend to be melodramatic.

Virgo: Favors accomplishment of details and commands from higher up. Focus on health, hygiene, and daily schedules.

Libra: Favors cooperation, compromise, social activities, beautification of surroundings, balance, and partnership.

Scorpio: Increases awareness of psychic power. Favors activities requiring intensity and focus. People tend to brood and become secretive under this moon sign.

Sagittarius: Encourages flights of imagination and confidence. This moon sign is adventurous, philosophical, and athletic. Favors expansion and growth.

Capricorn: Develops strong structure. Focus on traditions, responsibilities, and obligations. A good time to set boundaries and rules.

Aquarius: Rebellious energy. Time to break habits and make abrupt change. Personal freedom and individuality are the focus.

Pisces: The focus is on dreaming, nostalgia, intuition, and psychic impressions. A good time for spiritual or philanthropic activities.

Glossary of Magical Terms

Altar: A table that holds magical tools as a focus for spell workings.

Athame: A ritual knife used to direct personal power during workings or to symbolically draw diagrams in a spell. It is rarely, if ever, used for actual physical cutting.

Aura: An invisible energy field surrounding a person. The aura can change color depending on the state of the individual.

Balefire: A fire lit for magical purposes, usually outdoors.

Casting a circle: The process of drawing a circle around oneself to seal out unfriendly influences and raise magical power. It is the first step in a spell.

Censer: An incense burner. Traditionally a censer is a metal container, filled with incense, that is swung on the end of a chain.

Censing: The process of burning incense to spiritually cleanse an object.

Centering yourself: To prepare for a magical rite by calming and centering all of your personal energy.

Chakra: One of the seven centers of spiritual energy in the human body, according to the philosophy of yoga.

Charging: To infuse an object with magical power.

Circle of protection: A circle cast to protect oneself from unfriendly influences.

Crystals: Quartz or other stones that store cleansing or protective energies.

Deosil: Clockwise movement, symbolic of life and positive energies.

Deva: A divine being according to Hindu beliefs; a devil or evil spirit according to Zoroastrianism.

Direct/retrograde: Refers to the motion of a planet when seen from the earth. A planet is "direct" when it appears to be moving forward from the point of view of a person on the earth. It is "retrograde" when it appears to be moving backward.

Dowsing: To use a divining rod to search for a thing, usually water or minerals.

Dowsing pendulum: A long cord with a coin or gem at one end. The pattern of its swing is used to answer questions.

Dryad: A tree spirit or forest guardian.

Fey: An archaic term for a magical spirit or a fairylike being.

Gris-gris: A small bag containing charms, herbs, stones, and other items to draw energy, luck, love, or prosperity to the wearer.

Mantra: A sacred chant used in Hindu tradition to embody the divinity invoked; it is said to possess deep magical power.

Needfire: A ceremonial fire kindled at dawn on major Wiccan holidays. It was traditionally used to light all other household fires.

Pentagram: A symbolically protective five-pointed star with one point upward.

Power hand: The dominant hand; the hand used most often.

Scry: To predict the future by gazing at or into an object such as a crystal ball or pool of water.

Second sight: The psychic power or ability to foresee the future.

Sigil: A personal seal or symbol.

Smudge/smudge stick: To spiritually cleanse an object by waving smoke over and around it. A smudge stick is a bundle of several incense sticks.

Wand: A stick or rod used for casting circles and as a focus for magical power.

Widdershins: Counterclockwise movement, symbolic of negative magical purposes, sometimes used to disperse negative energies.

Spell Notes

Spell Notes

Spell Notes

Spell Notes

Llewellyn's 2016 Witches' Calendar

Captivating original artwork and a rich array of content have made *Llewellyn's Witches' Calendar*—now in its eighteenth year—the top-selling calendar of its kind. Enjoy new, enchanting scratch-board illustrations by award-winning artist Kathleen Edwards. Each month also offers an inspiring article, plus a spell or ritual. Discover love potions and poppets in February, sip the season's spirits in October, and make a solstice wish in December. Astro-logical data and magical correspondences are also included.

978-0-7387-3402-6, 28 pp., 12 x 12 $13.99

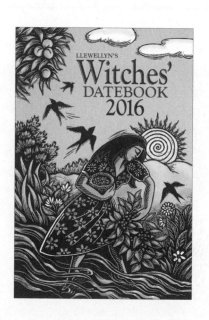

Llewellyn's 2016 Witches' Datebook

Keep up with the increasing busyness of life—both magical and mundane—with *Llewellyn's Witches' Datebook*, now featuring enchanting illustrations from award-winning artist Kathleen Edwards. Add a little magic to each day and keep pace with the ever-turning Wheel of the Year with this indispensable, on-the-go tool.

Find fresh ways to celebrate the sacred seasons and enhance your practice with seasonal spells (Deborah Blake), inspiring Sabbat musings (James Kambos), tasty Sabbat recipes (Susan Pesznecker), and Moon rituals (Elizabeth Barrette). Astrological information and daily colors are included for spellwork.

978-0-7387-3400-2, 144 pp., 5¼ x 8 $11.99

To order, call 1-877-NEW-WRLD
Prices subject to change without notice
Order at Llewellyn.com 24 hours a day, 7 days a week!

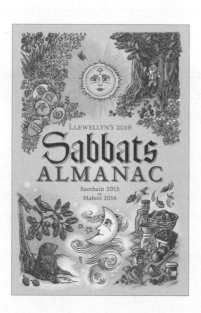

Llewellyn's 2016 Sabbats Almanac

Samhain 2015 to Mabon 2016

Make the most of each season of the Witches' year with *Llewellyn's Sabbats Almanac*. Packed with rituals, rites, recipes, and crafts, this essential guide offers fun and fresh ways to celebrate the eight sacred Wiccan holidays—and enrich your spiritual life throughout the year.

Get a unique perspective on honoring the Wheel of the Year from your favorite Wiccan and Pagan authors. Plan spiritually uplifting celebrations and sustainable seasonal activities. Perform Sabbat-specific rituals and family activities. Whip up tasty treats and crafts as reminders of the season's gifts and lessons. Also featured are astrological influences to help you plan rituals according to cosmic energies.

978-0-7387-3398-2, 312 pp., 5¼ x 8 $12.99

LLEWELLYN'S 2016

MAGICAL ALMANAC

PRACTICAL MAGIC
FOR EVERYDAY LIVING

Llewellyn's 2016 Magical Almanac
Practical Magic for Everyday Living

Filled with practical spells, rituals, and fresh ideas, *Llewellyn's Magical Almanac* has been inspiring all levels of magical practitioners for over twenty years.

This edition features nearly three dozen compelling articles, grouped by element, on elemental angels, quick Sabbat acknowledgments (instead of full rituals), copper energy rods, gem elixers, vision boards to transform energy, bubble magic, the magic of twin souls, photos for magical manifestation, and much more.

Also included is a handy calendar section— shaded for easy "flip to" reference—featuring world festivals, holidays, and 2016 Sabbats. You'll also find astrological information, plus incense and color correspondences, to empower your magical work.

978-0-7387-3405-7, 336 pp., 5¼ x 8 $11.99

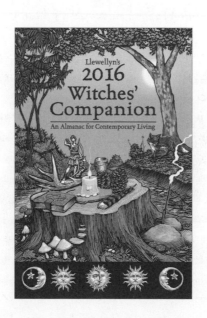

Llewellyn's 2016 Witches' Companion
An Almanac for Contemporary Living

Live your Craft every day with *Llewellyn's Witches' Companion*. This indispensable guide will keep you one step ahead of the latest witchy trends, Craft practices, and Pagan issues.

This year's edition is filled with wry and thought-provoking essays—transitioning to a Pagan lifestyle, lessons in kindness from the grasshopper and the ant, Pagan Standard Time, witchy ways of eating, banishing and polarization, magick spells for kids, recognizing and combating the evil eye, a guide to smudging, creating your own magical moniker, and much more.

Also featured is a sixteen-month calendar and lunar information to fuel your spellwork and rituals.

978-0-7387-3401-9, 288 pp., 5¼ x 8 $11.99